The Axiomatic Self

A coherent architecture for modeling reality

JOSEPH WEINSTEIN

Print ISBN: 978-1-73238-346-3

eBook ISBN: 978-1-09830-234-4

TABLE OF CONTENTS

Introduction

"The beginning of wisdom is in the defining of terms"

- attributed to Socrates

I would like you to consider this published definition of a term in philosophy:

"Ontology (introduced in 1606) is the philosophical study of the nature of being, becoming, existence, or reality, as well as the basic categories of being and their relations.[1] Traditionally listed as a part of the major branch of philosophy known as metaphysics, ontology often deals with questions concerning what entities exist or may be said to exist and how such entities may be grouped, related within a hierarchy, and subdivided according to similarities and differences. A very simple definition of ontology is that it is the examination of what is meant by 'being'." Wikipedia

If you, the reader, are like me, having an active interest in philosophy, would you agree with me that there are many philosophical definitions that seem over-wide, over-vague, and over-promising? When we first encounter definitions like these, we credulously and optimistically read in to them what we think they might mean, hoping we can become an 'insider' later by following them till more of their meaning becomes clear later? That in those cases we initially either have no pointed questions, too many of them, or that we dismiss our uncertainty or cognitive dissonance as a symptom of our philosophic ignorance and take faith in the assumed authority and coherence of the author?

I find that if I apply and require definitional exactitude for all terms from the start, I find many current or still widely respected philosophic themes and paths become ultimately only marginally helpful, if that. Some of them, so examined with clear common English definitions required become untenably flaccid with opacities, artistic license, and colloquialities. I freely see that for some others, these philosophical 'schools' seem to be a ready and welcome warren of engaging puzzles and complexity for fans and 'wan gestalters' who convivially (for the most part) take turns making 'gestures' with the terms and tenets, for polite and temporary non-demanding musing, like philosophical Karaoke. Of course each is entitled to his own entertainments, but I have no taste for such wafting indeterminate focus, certainly not here for this book...

With this book I am presenting an ontology, and *I will **define*** 'ontology' more narrowly and exactly for my purposes.

"An ontology is a way one conceptually classifies, subdivides and relates the perceived elements of reality". In computer science and information science, an ontology encompasses a representation, formal naming and definition of the categories, properties and relations between the concepts, data and entities that substantiate one, many or all domains of discourse. This is closer to mine than others, but when I use the term, I intend my definition.

You, the reader (especially as a reader who would be drawn to such a book) are emphatically not a tabula rasa. You already have your own ontology, how you look and think about reality, and you wield it daily in your navigation of life. In fact you may have several ontologies! Ontologies need not even intend to be catholic (small 'c', meaning 'all encompassing'). One person may hold and use multiple ontologies, switching back and forth from one view to another based on the persons' agenda or problem of the moment. Ontologies may conflict, or they may be totally orthogonal, or they might be practical subsets of a possible whole, each a useful shorthand for dealing with reality 'at that level'.

For instance we can consider the Dewey Decimal System to be an ontology of books, wherein they are classified arguably/roughly by content. There can certainly be other valid ontologies of books! If you are a system designer for Amazon, you may rightly design your own ontology of books that not only classifies books according to their content, differently than Dewey, but the Amazon ontology will have additional qualities/parameters for a book, including its publisher, availability, price etc. The U.S. Postal Service may have its own narrow ontology of books that would likely be orthogonal to either of those, wherein books are classified more simply by size and weight, and the wise and practiced (and proudly illiterate?) U.S.P.S. packager may know from the long successes of his work and his reliable ontology of books, that when all the dust settles, 'books' are really no different than any other non-hazardous non-fragile delivery product. ;)

If we compare the two common geometrical ways to map space; a Cartesian coordinate mapping, and a Polar coordinate mapping, these are alternative ontologies of location. A geometrist wielding either of those systems may come to the exact same answers to the same questions about space, but for each specific question, one or other of those views may make the solution much easier to find and express, or much more cumbersome. Thus depending on the sorts of questions you may have about reality, one ontology may seem immediate and ripe for your perusal while another approach, even if ultimately exactly equal in scope and fullness may forever seem like grey tedious homework, or worse. Beware, that aesthetes are not shy about conflating distaste with incorrectness or even evil. Historically such personal aesthetic and agenda-based judgments about world view approaches have blown up into wide and deadly political rifts.

While I cannot presume to meet every anonymous readers aesthetic tastes, purposes and standards, I hope to make the base of the ontology I am going to present from entirely clear and logically defensible definitions, hard axioms and assertions, and in cases where logical proofs are absent/impossible, I intend to be explicit about where any items of faith must be faced, accepted or rejected as tenets, accepting that as we proceed, that we are necessarily unsure, either way we go, at least until/if we can logically prove/provide a surety, or in the manner of Gödel, proving we can never know.

So, I present this described ontology as a candidate for addition to your own existing philosophical quiver/toolbox. I find it powerful and *predictive*. I find it to be fore-ordaining of the failures or conclusions of some other philosophic and scientific views and endeavors, clearing the way for others, unobfuscating some important questions.

I will try to define all the terms, clearly during their first use, and intend that they remain as defined throughout the book, except for occasional looser colloquial use of a given term when that is common, and to denote such in those cases. And this discipline is not a mere personal fastidiousness, or generous courtesy. It is a fundamental and repeated issue that in philosophical debate I find quite a few ontologies and positions, some long held and revered, *exist and survive* only by reliance on the aesthetics and plausibility of some of their concepts, hinted at and half-defined in soft-focus language that evaporates clinically but clearly into nothing when rigorous clear and consistent definitions are demanded. Some beautiful illusions survive on poetic license. Illusions can be dangerous. Thus, art is not innocent.

As Doctor Phil says, "Do you want to be right, or do you want to be happy?". This is a serious question, and for the purposes of this book, I intend to choose 'right' over 'happy'.

Absolutely, for a human life, it is certainly arguable that over-all, taking a biased-to-happy view may in some cases be better socially, individually and finally, rather than demanding/bearing an exacting logical doubt on every speculative issue or assumption. This is especially apt in the many cases where the person and society have utterly no practical means to benefit from the truth, and that there is no added harm in holding the falsehood. In the big scheme, truth is the lesser, a tool as needed when relevant, for the motivating core, ones' agenda/desires.

With the burgeoning success and reach of science, the goal posts of what the mix and minimum daily requirement of truth is, are certainly shifting, causing political flux worldwide between those who are ready and empowered by new truths, and those whose rationale for their accustomed happinesses are eroded by new truths, sooner and in greater proportion to their receiving any compensating powers and happinesses from those new truths. And we are not easy-erase whiteboards. There is a significant degree of cultural imprinting that is not as fungible/fluid as a philosopher-king might wish. A person's life, happiness, social status, and career may be based on one of these established aesthetic/ontological stances. To extend on Upton Sinclair, "It is difficult to get a man to understand something, when his salary, happiness, long-cherished world view, or social status depends upon his not understanding it". An accomplished and revered bull-fighter or trophy hunter may respect the tastes, intelligence and motives of people who give them this status, well over those who would present new or alternate moral or ecological values/

aesthetics, even if they considerately suggest that he/she might alternately become a winning tennis star. This resulting social viscosity of view/values might be over-pessimistically expressed by extending Planck's quip: "Science and social change advances one funeral at a time"...

And I will show that fundamental political change is won, not by logic, but by beauty contest, in the most heart-breaking and most deeply serious meaning of that term. I will show that logic is initially nothing but a pawn in the hands of combatants, and only comes into fungible discourse after the competing beauties have won their respective importances, identically in the eyes of all the unresolved parties.

This book is dedicated to my wife Leslie Hope Green, who has spared no effort or concern to keep me alive and happy, in times of great stress. This book would not exist, and I would have lived a much shorter, less accomplished life without her. Thank her too if you enjoy this.

And special thanks go to those I've had suffer while reading my not-yet-ready material, who nevertheless encouraged me and gave valuable feedback:

Joshua Rasmussen

David Lang

Peter Aborn

Steve Sapir

Max Weinstein, my son, who managed the project to develop the cover art

Chapter 1

The Core Separation, Objective and Subjective

"Everything should be as simple as it can be, but not simpler"

- attributed to Einstein

This ontology, this scheme of categorization, is a Dualism, in that it recognizes two distinct and separate 'halves of the sky', two disparate arenas of reality, and that they must each stand, and stand utterly apart, as equals. I will describe how there are many people who choose to see/categorize reality from only one or other of these two perspectives, an yet others whose world view contains a jumbled pastiche of both, but that from this dualist perspective, it will become clear and empowering to the reader that there are flaws and jeopardies in either of the two simpler non-dualist approaches, and that while each of them are understandable and promising to their adherents, particularly for their philosophic motivation to unify/simplify reality as/into one, and each of these simpler stances is in fact strong in the area where it is apt, I will show that either alone is doomed, fundamentally, by being over-simple. A reader should now be empowered to efficiently drill toward the fatal flaws in any such over-simple world views.

Here are the two core definitions that are the crux of this book, on which we will build.

Subjective - Any thing that depends on a mind/consciousness in order for that thing to exist.

Objective - Any thing that exists independently of any mind/consciousness.

There are certainly other, more colloquial or broader or fuzzier definitions of these two terms, but *for the purposes of this ontology, these are the exact meanings*. In the rigorous context of this view, any other intent of those words should be expressed otherwise and clearly. I will show examples.

Here I will supply other definitions of 'objective', to make my operant definition as exactly understood as possible, and to show credence and understanding for other popularly used/assumed definitions of the term.

1. Objective as above, and also including the 'mind invariant'. For example, mathematical proofs can be said to deliver objective results, in that no matter who (what mind)

accurately follows the logic of the proof, they will arrive at the same answer. So the answer is mind invariant, provably the same for everyone who is coherent in this regard. From my most restrictive definition of 'objective', all assertions, which include mathematical ones, are statements of language, and as assertions, require an asserter (no math without mathematicians etc), so I would most strictly say that such assertions are subjective *and* mind-invariant, though still mind-dependent. However, we may well want to declare logically provable assertions/truths as 'objective' for the parlance and purposes of some arguments and discourse.

2. Objective like the rules of chess. Here, something is 'objective' because it is unambiguously described and is intended to be unargued. This is a declared/enforced/assumed *consensus*. There is nothing inherently immutable about the rules of chess, and in fact they have varied over time. But at a given instant, they are considered 'objective' by those that would defend the status quo rules against any question or effort to change them or disagree with them. So, this third-level 'objective' is essentially a voluntary adherence to a consensus.

3. Perceived consensus 'objectivity'. There can be cases where a constituency may agree on an 'objective fact' which is nevertheless false, such as those who believe(d)/knew/agreed that the Sun revolves around the Earth. There are plenty of currently popularly believed falsehoods. These people also have a consensus and may use the term 'objective'.

4. Consensuses of one. There may be a society whose members will share an explicit belief/statement that is taken/declared as 'objective', but when/if pressed to clarify and define the terms in the belief, none of these people will even agree on premises and terms. This is a sort of objectivity by/of desire.

The exactly mutually exclusive definitions of 'subjective' and 'objective' as I define them form two absolute, logically, mathematically disjoint sets. As defined, and adhering to logical coherency, these two sets are catholic in their union: every single thing, utterly anything abstract, imaginary, or concrete that is part of your inner or outer reality, falls into one of these sets *exclusively or* into the other. Nothing is in neither, and nothing is in both. This splits your reality into two.

I refer to logical coherency early on, as a required discipline, even when it will expose disconcerting ramifications. This is because our absolute adherence to logic will, from this book's perspective, expose fatal flaws in some deeply held world views. I have engaged more than one deep and protracted debate on philosophic perspectives, where when I ultimately clarified our differences sufficiently distilled and focused to logical inconsistency/incoherence in their position, the counterpart finally and openly renounced logic itself rather than abandon or further question his position. One then argued that "logic is limiting", and would not recognize/accept its chafing confinement for the specific issue! Beware of fair-weather logicians.

He was of course absolutely right. Logic is limiting, intendedly so. The *purpose* of logic is to limit. It is a filter for incoherence, whether inadvertent or purposeful, with no quarter given or possible, no matter how historically enshrined the towers that may fall. Clear communication, even to ones self, requires coherency.

Communion and love, on the other hand, are quite possible without any intellectually expressible basis, as when the members of a congregation of any sort presume rightly or wrongly, that they all already know the truth. We/They may sway together in perfect rhythm, sharing the knowing, caring gazes of bonding, giving and accepting the merest gestures and utterances as shorthand confirmations of what they/we already know. We've seen this, we've experienced it, in churches, political rallies and rock concerts and family dinners. This can be awesomely powerful, galvanizing, and truly beautiful (though not immune from danger), but for the narrow and exacting purposes of this book, which is to transmit new ideas clearly, completely, and defensibly, especially to those who may be at first (and maybe to the last) ill-disposed to them, full and explicit logical coherency is key.

These two sets divide reality into utterly separate universes, not abutting areas with a tasteful privacy fence between them, with some things close to the fence being more like the other side, nothing ever switching sides etc. From the pure perspective of either the subjective or objective realms (space-times), I will show that the very existence of the other is hypothetical at best. They remain utterly, eternally, and logically necessarily, by definition separate.

As I alluded before, from this dualist perspective, there are the two main classifications of over-simple alternative ontologies, and they exactly relate to the two core definitions. We have what I will call the 'objective reductionists', those who attempt to ultimately reduce/constrain all of reality to the objective realm (materialism is a common term). The symmetric and opposing tack is for the 'subjective reductionists', those who attempt to ultimately reduce all of reality to the conscious/subjective. The former are historically newer, displaying more Western scientism, while the latter have a much longer history, and are often religion/spirituality-based. We will address each of these camps more deeply and their respective problems later, but for now, we can expect that any such attempts will reduce, co-opt, 'explain away', subjugate or deny the independent reality of the other.

Chapter 2

What Goes Where?

Now let's do a quick stab at guessing into which of the two sets each of any of our 'things' will go. And in due consideration for would-be reductionists of either stripe, let us see if there is any way we can make either of them correct, such as if either's 'opposing set' is provably empty!

My definitions have so far presumed the definition of mind/consciousness. Even before assaying a rigorous definition, and in fact independently of it, simply by the very definition of 'subjective' I have posited, the subjective set gains its inaugural member, mind/consciousness itself. Tautologically, for all X, X depends on the existence of X, in order that X exist. If/when there is a mind, an instance of consciousness, the subjective set is not empty.

As to the definition of consciousness (and everything else!), we must start from the subjective perspective. This is because this is where we live, experientially, proximally in our subjective space-time. First, we experience. Our interpretation of our experience, follows, most often done intuitively, subconsciously and well within sub-second speed. We see the raw flashes of light and movement of shapes, hear the sounds, and interpret them into something plausible and integral with our current world view. For those readers who may bear any doubt of the existence of mind/consciousness, I cite you, the reader, not as a human body in the objective world, but solely you at the center of your consciousness, the private focus and recipient of your raw experiences, as an axiomatic example of mind/consciousness. Details, obviously will follow.

Here is a philosophy 101 topic whose ramifications will become crucial, so I bring it up now:

Sol·ip·sism: the view or theory that the self is all that can be known to exist. – Google Dictionary

Solipsism; from Latin solus, meaning 'alone', and ipse, meaning 'self') is the philosophical idea that only one's mind is sure to exist. As an epistemological position, solipsism holds that knowledge of anything outside one's own mind is unsure; the external world and other minds cannot be known and might not exist outside the mind. – Wikipedia

Philosophy may even subdivide solipsism; there is *metaphysical solipsism*, which is pure subjective reductionism, the precipitate position that there *is* in fact nothing but the self.

The core apt-and-wise challenge of Solipsism, is that it puts a high logical standard for 'can be known'. We can never logically prove/verify that any experience we have, any interpretation of any of our sensory inputs or imaginations, is anything more than the private experience in your mind! Anything more than an internal construct/imagination. Any and all such could be your self-generated (albeit *very imaginative* :)) dream. This goes far beyond the typical 'brain-in-a-bucket' analogy. Here, there is no brain, no bucket. If logic be upheld, it is possible, and utterly un-disprovable that you are the *only* mind, factually disembodied except when/if you should choose to imagine one, you the largely unself-aware, solitary God, imagining absolutely everything, and that absolutely nothing has or needs any existence or substance except as/while you are imagining it. No real 'we', no communion. 'We others' are also all merely figments of your imagination!

The *metaphysical solipsist* is logically precipitate, in error, because even though all he/she can know is self/experience, that does not and cannot deliver proof that non-experiential things may nevertheless exist. It is just by definition that they are ever unknowable because they are inexperienceable, they are not experiences. But you, if you want to be a subjective reductionist, and retain the intellectual honesty, an exacting fealty to logic, you can declare as a fundamental matter of faith that you believe there to be nothing else. You cannot be logically faulted, but the ultimate logical ramifications are dire (for most tastes...), that you lose essentially **everything but yourself**, No God except you. and no one, nothing except the imaginary ones you create/experience in your dreams. This 'Self As Deity' (SAD) model of reality declares *zero* externalities, zero objectivities, zero that is not 'of self'. It is the ultimate declaration of independence, separation, isolation. This SAD model of reality is self-consistent logically, and no logic can definitively prove or disprove it. We have only our circumstantial statistical suspicions and our aesthetic revulsion (to most but not all of us!) to disparage/dislike this model. The SAD model is eternally occupiable, if not safe/sure. Baldly, it's probability of truth is eternally non-zero. The crucial corollary is that *any other alternative model of reality*, particularly and exactly in so far as a model posits some/any externality/objectivity/other-than-self within it, that *no such alternative model of reality can ever attain logical surety either*. Reason cannot deliver exact and full logical surety, and mathematically so, because there is always at least that one SAD alternative taking up some fraction of possibility.

Understand that in either case, because we are presented this early and fundamental block from logical certainty, we have a first leap of faith to make, that we will never logically obviate. We must decide whether to postulate and follow on faith, as a working hypothesis, that there is an objective realm out there, independent and separate from our(your!) perceptions, or *symmetrically-and-oppositely guess* that there is not. I choose devoutly to operate with the presumption that there is an objective half of reality.

"Ceci n'est pas une pipe." - Magritte

This was a brilliant warning to distinguish image from reality, and is apt and useful at this time. You may think you know an apple or a pipe, and that it is a physical thing, so you and it 'are in the objective world'. No. For every objective thing posited/pondered, there are two things: your subjective idea/model/image of the thing, and the presumed/projected real thing, still out there and obdurately separate, independent of your or anyone's perception..

Your mental model of the apple may include many relevant-to-you imagined-and-remembered qualities, visual, tactile, olfactory, biochemical etc, but from the objective perspective, the infinitude of subatomic and in-motion biologic realities of any real apple are simply numerically beyond comprehension, let alone their interacting changing details and subtleties, and that is if the apple really exists! You may easily ponder an apple you had in a lunch box years ago, or a hypothetical suspected object like a GPA (Greatest Possible Apple ;)). Your subjective universe is absolutely real to you, as are its contents, but it remains factually separate from objective reality we all (most all) attempt to model/mirror in our subjective space.

So, there is for most people a rich set of things we employ and integrate in our mental model of objective reality, which we intend to represent things that are out there in objective space-time. When studying/postulating about the objective realm, we must take on and retain the scientific intellectual chastity of doubt, precisely because this objective realm is remote from us, we each cloistered in our individual subjectivity with our models, all our ideas and tenets about this objective world must be couched as theories. Honorably, physics does this for even its most trusted and tested tenets. No matter how statistically 'lucky' we have been in predicting stuff with enough accuracy to visit the moon, and to have confidence in black holes etc, we can never *logically prove*, again, that any of it is real or that our imagery is true. No matter how statistically unlikely we may believe that the sun should not rise tomorrow, if it did not, it would our calculations that would be bereft.

Happily, the other hand, I will show that this requisite default doubt is not as much needed in the subjective realm, where there is much more logical certainty on tap.

Chapter 3

That You Are, Where You Are...

From a subjective perspective I assert that you, at the center of your consciousness, are axiomatic, and necessary, non-contingent, uncaused in that context, which is your first/proximal perspective. I have used some apologetics terms for a ring of familiarity for folks interested in that topic, and I may expand those later.

There are however, some approaches to reality that prefer to discount, denigrate, or actually deny the individual self. Some of these offer 'lack of evidence proofs' for their position, rightly saying that for instance, you are not your mind, you are not your memory, body etc, and asking what are you are, if not any of those those things. I will answer.

FIRST, WHERE YOU ARE.

To a first, and feeble-logic projection, the objective-and-sympa-thetic view is that 'you' are 'in your brain', associated with your body etc, but when pressed to actually define the active/receptive actor at the center of subjectivity, objective science cannot even define it, most harshly explaining it away as imaginary and an illusion, a 'side effect of biochemical reactions' etc. There were also the embarrassingly weak-and-missing-the-point Decartes 'in the pineal gland' stuff. But just as a movie's meaning will never be explained by the chemistry and physics of film, the objective scientist is bootless to directly address the subjective as such, as it lives, as it is. Western objective science rightly limits itself to what is, purified/isolated from any subjectivity. But this is not to say subjectivity is not real, just that it complicates the subject being pursued. It could be said that between subjectivity and objectivity, physics just took the easier problem space. So, where you are really?

Now please, for a moment, imagine a simple geometric cube in your mind. Those light grey lines for the edges, in front of your unpopulated darker background... Rotate it around a bit, like an idle examination of a rubix cube, then have it rest stationary for now... Now arbitrarily deem it to be of a specific dimension, such as a one-foot cube, an inch, a mile, any linear unit you like or invent. Now, geometrically from a careful measurement of the apparently differing angles and differing lengths due to perspec-tive, you can now mathematically and exactly *calculate where you are*, the viewer in this experience, at your *point of view*, relative to that cube, looking at it. The first attribute of you in subjective space is locality. You are at the center, you occupy your point of view. This locating/relativity is strictly in subjective space. It says nothing and can mean nothing about anything in that hypothetical and utterly separate other space, the space of the moon and stars, the physical universe. But you're there, in your subjective space-time. For a bonus effect, instead of rotating this imaginary cube of yours in your mind, assay/consider it to be fixed in place, while you take it upon yourself to do the moving, taking you and your point of view up and over, and back under the cube till you return to your original place. Relatively, geometrically there should be do difference, yet I'll wager the latter exercise was more troublesome, even queasy-making. There is something of gravity at you.

But you cannot look at your own real, current self at your point of view, you must infer it, yourself. To view something requires separation, perspective, and you cannot distance yourself from your operant self. You cannot simultaneously see it and be it. You can certainly and easily model a disembodied viewer observing an imagined cube, for instant, and do the calculations, for fun. But the real you is creating/observing the model. You are not currently at that location relative to the one-cubit cube.

Now, imagine you are in a lightless, windowless vault, with only a flashlight to find the tools and means to make your escape. The one tool you will never illuminate is the flashlight itself! You must infer its location by following the projected cone of light back to its focus/origin. Consider your conscious living attention like that beam from a flashlight, that you train on subjects of your interest. There you are, beaming/looking out from the point of origin, that exact point of view.

"I exist" The First Axiom Of The Articulate* Consciousness

"But do I really exist?"

  "Who wants to know?" ;)

*(For the purposes of asserting this axiom, I assume/require that the consciousness in question has the linguistic ability to articulate an axiom, or actually just make any assertion)

The following is a slightly prolix and legalistic exposition, because I penned it originally to withstand and dispense all attacks from an arguer who was very intelligent and yet fervently bound to a philosophy denying the self, ultimately and illogically himself, even as his every protestation belied his non-existence!

First, some definitions:

5. a claimer/stater/proposer

A claimer/stater/proposer is anyone who can/does make a claim, make a statement. This is a trivial, obvious definition. It is included specifically to illustrate and declare that any other specificity or details about the claimant are moot and irrelevant to the following thesis. This is to forefend any question like "Who is this claimant?" as irrelevant as long as it is a stater, as defined/evidenced. You may comfortably presume/assume them to be a natural human, or if it suits you, your presumed set of proposers could include any more 'exotic' disembodied consciousness or talking crystals you may posit or imagine. For the purposes of this argument, all we care about is that he/she/it has the ability to utter a claim.

6. Defining 'axiom'

"An axiom is an irreducible primary. It doesn't rest upon anything else in order to be valid, and it cannot be proven by any "more basic" premises. A true axiom can not be refuted because the act of trying to refute it requires that very axiom as a premise. An attempt to contradict an axiom can only end in a contradiction." (copied gratefully from http://www.importanceofphilosophy.com/Metaphysics_Axiom.html) This is a current, most philosophically rigorous definition, not for instance Euclid's softer usage, which boiled down to "anything I claim as true that I won't/can't discuss/doubt/deny".

The Assertion: "I exist" is an axiom.

"I exist" is axiomatically true proposition, whenever proposed, at a minimum for the duration of the utterance, the utterer being self-evidently extant, identified necessarily and sufficiently, even if only to their self, as the proposer. "I exist" doesn't rest on anything else to be valid, and it requires its being true (the existence of the claimer) just to be claimed, and it cannot be tested/proven by anything more basic, nor can it be contradicted by the claimant. You can't doubt yourself, because *there you are* in that incongruous attempt, the one doing the doubting. "Do I exist?" "Who wants to know?" ;) You can't test yourself because you're the one running the test, and can't even pretend to escape yourself for any temporary suspension of belief that a test would require. Even the cop in the "Three Stooges" looking for them in a dark cave when he called out "Is there anyone in there?" didn't buy it when Curly gave an emphatic "No!" ;)

Regarding "at a minimum for the duration of the utterance", that is the temporal bounds of the context in which the axiom is axiomatic. There is no claim or requirement that the proposer will continue to exist for any period beyond the utterance, nor any claim or requirement that the claimant existed for any time before making the claim. While obviously and usually our set of claimers are natural humans who spend most of their time not claiming anything but still exist, any/all particular circumstances of the claimers are irrelevant to the axiom.

I was helpfully referred to Quine's objection regarding axioms, that the singling out of any subset of statements within a theory as axioms/axiomatic is conventional, other statements could be chosen with the same effect, given sufficient implicational rear-rangements within the theory. I disagree, and clarify: I am not singling anything out. An ontology, by virtue solely of it's defini-tion may passively-but-logically connote a set of strong axioms, to be discovered rather than any limited selective anointment/enshrinement. Ie: no 'convention' allowed, all axioms, known or yet to be discovered, deemed so by meeting the exacting and neutral standard set by the definition of 'axiom'. For Quine to use the term 'conventional' is to permit a softer definition of 'axiom', such as Euclid's, where some presuppositions are titled 'axioms' to cosset them as 'no-touch-me' elements for which the author will simply brook no question.

MORE DEFINITIONS:

Tautology - a phrase or expression in which the same thing is said twice in different words. I would distinguish this from another definition, which is "an expression which is true in all cases" or "a statement that is true by necessity or by virtue of its logical form". The distinction is that these latter definitions would include axioms as tautologies. But as long as there is no pejorative to 'tautology', the distinction may be held moot.

To exist is vastly more elemental than the ability to claim so, let alone the actual act of claiming so. "to exist is to be existing" is tautological and unhelpful, but to exist and to simply affirmatively claim so, is emphatically not. The axiom is made once, and makes no specious equation.

I bring up these latter codicils because I've had some fervent attempts to deny the claim of axiomaticity. It has been said that the axiom "requires that proposers don't exist, then they only exist while they propose something, then disappear". True, but not damaging nor pejorative. In your periods of silence you retain an identity, and may at any time re-utter a proposition, but if you and I are in a room, and neither of us is asserting anything, there are no asserters in the room.

I even had a challenge to define "I", something so intuitive that it merits no entry in some dictionaries! Here is one I found:

"I

[ahy]

1. the nominative singular pronoun, used by a speaker in referring to himself or herself. pronoun US ? /??/

I pronoun (PERSON) the person speaking"

As in the axiom, the 'I' is simply, sufficiently identified as the speaker of the claim. For the purposes of this post, the 'I' does not refer/require anything physical, such as the lips or brain, just the occupant of the mind, the active subjective agent, who may only be silently saying this in their head, to themselves. This is the subjective, conscious, psychological 'I'. Hard materialists may demean this 'I' as a 'convenient fiction', and so be it, even though they are illogically, finally denying themselves. The proposition makes no claim for what is true when/if there are no 'I's so defined, so the materialist still has no argument against the axiom:

1. If/when there is an 'I', and

2. if/when such an 'I' says "I exist" then

3. he/she is axiomatically correct.

You exist, now, unquestionably, axiomatically. In fact all subjective time and space depend on you. You are a-priori to any real (your) experience, and there is no real (your) subjective time without you there. You exist for all real subjective time, and are uncaused, necessary and a-priori for subjectivity. This should be the inexorable base of your self-confidence. Not omniscience, not omnipotence, but unquestionable existence, you, something there, more surely than *everything* else.

Chapter 4

When you are...

This question will highlight that the subjective space-time and objective space-time are logically, utterly separate, commensurate with their definitional rigor.

From a reasonable pedestrian external perspective (typical mix of objective assumptions and subjective assumptions), you, as an instance of consciousness, are presumed by an observer to 'inhabit' that body they identify you with, and are pedestrianly observed/presumed/projected to be conscious for hours, then not conscious for some hours, in a typical daily cycle. From the objective perspective, when you're dead asleep in bed (let's ignore dreaming for the moment), there is no 'you' as defined by consciousness, active subjectivity. Then in the morning you pop back up again like a daisy back on the objective social scene. But from a purely subjective perspective, and purely subjective time, you are always there! You're never, by axiom, able to experience any time when you are not in fact there, conscious to experience it. Yes, when we, most of us, normally work with the assumption of an objective universe with its time and space, we freely interpret and understand that the clock did not instantly switch ahead, nor did the sun turn on like a light in the *perceptual instant* between when you decided just to rest your 'eyes for a second during a TV commercial, and your very next perception of birds chirping just before re-opening your eyes to an apparent dawn. But if this episode were in a Samahdi isolation chamber, bereft of references to 'reset your objective clock', you could well accept, and might be correct that the shut-eye period was indeed just a moment of peace in an uninterrupted continuous time.

I have actually had a committed subjective reductionist, arguing against the reality of the objective realm, go so far as to assert that they are *never* unconscious, explaining away 'pre-them' times as simulations, and fossil hunts as just-in-time simulations, being generated as needed by the simulating mind!

For all your directly experienced (subjective) time, you are there necessarily, eternally from the perspective and duration of subjective reality. It is only in the wielding of the objective space hypothesis that you can model 'you not being there'.

And from an objective spacial perspective, to watch or be an athlete, to wield proprioception so accurately and fluently in dynamic kinesis, we see oneness with gravity and the physical world. But nevertheless, the athlete and we all, are really and impressively, *flying by instruments*! What we transparently and fluently interpret in our vision and hearing and balance as open windows on objective reality, are in fact no less 'screen data' than the myriad ones and zeros that physicists consume and interpret as 'false-color' photos of gas clouds and gravitational waves. Your 'eyesight' is no longer light, the image having been inverted by the eye, then converted to the encodings of nerve signals before you get it. The speed, bandwidth and practical signal fidelity of our senses are impressive, but they are data images none the less. Our perceived window on the world is a narrow near-real-time simulation/reconstruction. It is only our playing to our own interpretation that frees us subjectively into the objective universe.

The objective reductionist may now chime in, that this is all just imaginary, and he/she is right, except for their intended pejorative. To an objective reductionist, 'imaginary' means 'unreal'. But subjectively, to a real person (a consciousness), imagination is constructive, in fact the only constructivity.

And from a practical perspective, either from the objective or subjective perspective, 'imaginary' is all consciousness *has* to be! The power and freedom of our subjectivity is precisely the freedom/separation we subjectively have from the objective 'now', the inner alternative arena of focus, instead of being hard-wired to reactivity to raw external stimuli.

It is precisely our freedom to move back and forth in our subjective experience and space-time, in our constructed alternate realities, to dwell on and relive the past, and to imagine, rehearse and compare necessarily unreal imagined futures, that allows us to develop, compare, and follow long-term strategies, not merely always attending and reacting to the real-time input of the now.

It is the crucial power that we can specifically and tactically ignore the 'now' when we deem it distracting to our planned and plotted course/agenda toward our chosen and necessarily imagined future.

And I want to emphasize that this temporal emancipation is utterly and only subjective. The objective clock, and objective reality is still clicking inexorably forward, while you're paying attention or meditating on the past and or future, or out like a light, snoring in bed. When you look inward, imagining, you are investing objective time for inner peace, enjoyment, or planning, but objectively this is a risk too. Do check in with your senses and attend to objective reality occasionally, lest ye be taken unaware by a hungry lion or run over in a crosswalk by a city bus.

I will wax poetic/artistic for a smidge. Imagine achieved consciousness as a vector, a directed line escape, to a point of view at some achieved distance of perspective, standing off in darker imaginary space, vectored out from some point in a planet-colored hyperplane that represents your sensory window to objective reality. Your body is likely represented at that point of departure from that reality hyperplane from which you escaped, while your mind, in its freedom, is out away at that distal point.

More distance gives more perspective and more detachment, for better or worse (no easy answers/values).

Chapter 5

What/who you are. The spectrum of self

Now let us consider you functionally as the living, active/receptive heart of your subjectivity, you at your point of view. I hope it is clear when I say 'point of view' that I mean more and other than the colloquial sense of 'from your collection of opinions and experience'. I mean it as I described in chapter 3, it is where you look out and reside as the focus of your experience, at the geometric center of your subjective space-time.

Here, from the purely subjective perspective it must be entertaining and amazing that you fortuitously just happen to have a powerful and specific suite of potencies and facilities! You have some fairly constant seemingly hard-wired multi-sensory 'screen' of input from the 'now', that (maybe real?) outside. Further, and strangely (again from a purely subjective perspective) you also seem to be Bluetooth'ed to an animal out there, that you can remotely control, including limbs that you can wave in and out of your peripheral vision. Internally, you also amazingly have transparent access to memory and memories you populate, which record and order your experiences. This memory documents your chosen and observed constancies of your identity as you pass through time, and also showing the evolution of other aspects of your identity and your ideas.

You occupy a subjective mental space you can freely populate with a changing 'working set' selection of current, past or imaginary future objects and experiences, and you can freely ponder and focus on them, making them your temporary, exaggerated and simplified reality. I say it is exaggerated, distorted in proportion, because of your temporarily heightened and narrowed responsivity to this current self-selected view/subset of reality. To quote the genius Daniel Kahneman, "nothing in life is as important as while you are thinking about it." This exaggeration is a double-edged sword, useful as a magnifying glass, allowing you to do detailed observation and have tactically useful heightened reaction. On the other hand, it is exactly that heightened reaction that can be harmfully disproportionate with negative effects in a broader, long-term perspective.

Now it is time to discuss another faculty of yours, more crucial than these other tools. Most crucially to the value and utility of your entire subjectivity is a uniquely subjective and key dimension, for which there is utterly no counterpart in objective space-time:

You have glorious, simple, visceral, fundamentally motivating *aesthetics*! I thoroughly intend to elevate aesthetics, this ability of consciousness, from any wan science-denigrated notion like effete fashion. Aesthetics are the simple, animal, lower-than-language reactions and emotional(motivating) gut judgments of raw goodness/beauty or raw bad/ugly/fearful etc. We attach these our values to each image or idea or experience we have. This is the core animal ability to like, love, identify with, or fear, reject and hate, to directly, simply, and imperiously individually assign/associate a good/bad value on an otherwise neutral (as they all are) thing, circumstance, or idea. No interposed ratiocination is necessary or possible in your first aesthetic reaction/decision, just your welling joy or disdain. This core facility of yours will found the basis of all your motivations, morals and agenda. We share this power and awareness with all sentient life, certainly in common with our friends as far as the reptiles and octopuses. Needless to say, I will be expanding on this crucial subjective power later.

From an objective perspective, these facilities/potencies of yours are easily associated with various parts of the brain and body hardware. But as close as objectivity/science will come in documenting the wiring and workings of your *facilities*, it will ever remain unable to pinpoint or even define you, the central active/passive wielder/receptor of these tools and their inputs. From the objective perspective, Oliver Sacks has written fascinating books about people with initially confounding and inexplicable mental ailments, which come to be diagnosed as specific localized brain damage. In one case, an otherwise completely normal articulate functioning individual suffered and expressed the surety that everyone of his family had been abducted, and that they had been replaced by calculated and expert actors/substitutes. Why or how this could be done was as beyond him as it would to anyone he described it to, but it was viscerally true to him. An odd clue was that he was thoroughly and normally accepting that a phone call with his dad, for instance, was unquestionably simply to/with his dad, but not in person. It turns out that an accident this person had had, had severed a specific nerve between parts of the brain, and it appears that the brain channel that presents a visual image is paralleled by a totally separate nerve which appears to pass the aesthetic value that was attached to that image. It was this second nerve that had been severed, so this person suddenly got none of the warmth and love feelings that he'd expected from seeing his loved ones. The image itself was exact, but the sense of fakeness/impostors was his only way for him to rationalize his now being so emotionally unmoved by them.

So now, while I am paring away (distinguishing) these facilities of yours from what you are at the naked core, you will become smaller at that center, that point, abiding there, even if you are unaware, such as if your memory had been wrested(hypothetically/logically) from you. Yes, there is less doable, less meaningful, as we successively pare away our facilities from our self, but this mental exercise in isolating you is just temporary for the exact philosophic purpose, that you, the minimal 'denatured' self, abide, separate from all that you practically wield or know.

I will certainly expand on the bigger, fully equipped/outfitted you, you with your memory, your aesthetic judgments that serve as the foundation of your agenda and motivations, and your private space-time for your imagination. We will again build you up to become (return to) your full, beautiful and complex active motivated self, wherein you create and extend your operant identity, even beyond your individuality into a bigger social self/identity where we may commune.

The most fundamental facility we have is memory. We are not our memory/memories, but when we separate ourselves from memory, we lose so much, even the ability to sense time is gone. In order to sense time, one must have the memory to store a current image of reality (however small and specific), and the ability to then 'avert our eyes' internally, if only for creating an interceding experience as evidence of a quantum of time passing, then enough more memory to capture a second image of reality (and it may only be the image of a digital watch face), in order to compare the 'now' to the first image we took. Indeed our very perceived identity is, as I hinted above, only evidenced by certain aspects of what we observe and remember over time, some of those which stay constant while other things change. What are we without memory? I assert we are still there, the focus, the point of view, the recipient of experience, but unable to be self-aware, totally and transiently reactive, not reflective. I would equate this state with some of the very lowest life forms in the animal kingdom.

I think consciousness, from an objective perspective, is a quantity (not a binary true/false) tied to the amount of 'free read/write memory' available, the degree to which it allows the imaginary space, the 'number of pixels' available to detail an image, the amount of history that can be stored and retrieved, etc. And I'd expect that the biological investment in this memory is still bounded, because the bigger the temptation to be 'in your head', shuffling and playing your own created narratives instead of paying attention to the now, is still a biological risk, that you lost info or timely reactivity to the outside world, from which you must still eke a living.

I spoke of a spectrum of identity/self because your facilities, identifications, and attachments sit along a range of mutability, ranging from those which you individually cannot change, to those you will not change, to those you might, to those you regularly change, to those you change instant to instant. Particularly your instant-to-instant choice of conscious focus/exaggeration alters what you care about and how you react, ie: what/who you are at that moment, to a significant degree. Your body's heart rate, breathing, and adrenaline production will autonomously, measurably change with as random and small an event as the turn of a playing card, but thankfully only if/when you've temporarily invested your *self* in that card game. On the other end of the spectrum are your strongest social bonds, your core tenets of your world view, your visceral appreciation for food, etc, which you might entertain 'philosophic argument' but would mostly practically never doubt. However, there are cases where people have chosen to sacrifice deep, even vital values, knowingly giving their lives for another idea/value of their choosing. Your power over your values/identity is greater than you may ever need to exercise.

If you have 'free will' (another topic I will follow up) I propose that it is exactly in the degree of your freedom to choose/change your identity, your focus, your attachments/investments of self. It is in those rare, most conscious moments when you fundamentally decide to reprogram a serious article of your identity (and therefore agenda), that you transcend Pavlov and Skinner and are importantly, consciously self-determinant. Day to day, we mostly run on 'semi-auto pilot' with our current self-programming, identity and values. Like a lazy security guard, we casually glance at each first visceral reaction/instinct we have for every moment, and take it in unquestioned. This real-time annotated/valued imagery comes to us freely, unbidden, generated by our powerful, immediate, and rich subconscious reaction/interpretation engine, which effortlessly delivers the experience with a generated aesthetic evaluation according to your existing programming. We, as the lazy security guard, typically accept it at face value, as presented, waving it through and reacting to it unquestioningly as the truth, including its assigned goodness/badness with respect to our values, our aesthetics, our agenda. And mostly this is for the best, and what we share with all sentient animals as a prime survival skill. Self-pondering can fatally get in the way of a quick reaction.

Practically, instant-to-instant you are what you love, your values, what you've programmed into your autopilot reaction engine. You will react quickly and automatically in those interests with no need for fastidious and articulated clarity. You may certainly rationalize your behavior(s) after (or during) the fact if language/thought is needed at all, but the reaction, as cleverly nuanced as it may have been, was a *reaction*, primarily produced subconsciously. Indeed, all animals, we included, have survived more surely by this fluent visceral reactivity than by articulated reason. A mother cat can react with powerful and instant 'moral authority' and acumen when her kittens are threatened. She knows what is good and bad in this scenario, and a hundred pound dog had better not be in the bad column at that instant. Where you, the evolved human higher consciousness, are truly most fully conscious/active is actually in those rarer, limited, and effortful times when you temporarily separate yourself from your rich instinct/gut/intuitions, and instead consciously invest/risk in a pause, calling a timeout on reality, where you become an alert 'reality guard', and take a step back (investing the time/delay) and do a diligent audit/review of the facts, what your subconscious likely story engine has delivered, and what your current relevant motivations/opinions/aesthetics really are.

If I am to recommend one book to anyone interested in the mind, it would be "Thinking, Fast and Slow" By Kahneman. Among the myriad of brilliant insights this book offers, he makes tested distinctions between the always-on rich and powerful plausibility engine in our subconscious, and the slow, feebly limited and effortful 'executive consciousness', and the ramifications of their use. Kahneman's career is in testing/proving and helping minimize the predictable *systematic* logical errors that humans make in their decision processes, that provably hamper their life goals. One fascinating result was in his giving people logic problems to solve, with the people sorted/categorized in two ways, by IQ according to standard tests, and separately by whether they were more religious or less. These are people who at a given IQ level, all solved neutral IQ-type questions equally. The following experiment questions were categorized in two ways, how intellectually easy or hard they were to solve, and whether the question had an intuitively obvious plausible answer. This test revealed a single, intriguing systematic difference, which was at every one of the IQ ranges covering the spectrum, between the religious and non-religious. For all questions with no quick and apparent answer, everyone at a level worked for, and got comparable results, but specifically and only in the case of questions that were hard, still solvable, and which had an apparent, plausible but *false* answer, it was the religious that more often chose the wrong-but-plausible answer. The equally intelligent non-religious more often assayed the extra doubt and effort to calculate and find the actual answer, more often escaping the tempting trap of trusting their gut reaction.

Chapter 6

On Morality

MY DEFINITION OF MORALITY:

Morality is manifested in someone's conscious, voluntary, personal sacrifice, motivated simply to benefit others of equal or lesser relevant fortune, with no recompense expected, instead motivated ultimately solely by the givers aesthetic attachment, their love/respect/care for the recipients. Thus morality is based on the givers intent, motivated by pure aesthetics.

THE PARTS:

Conscious - Morality is the pinnacle product and utility of aesthetics, as the motivator in the social context. Morality is a judgment/quality assigned to *intent* of the actor.

Note immediately that the intent is logically distinct from the effect, distinct from any actual social benefit. For instance, we all benefit socially from adhering to traffic laws and minding speed bumps etc, but those things are not moral. Those things bear no intent themselves. Nor are benefits themselves moral! Benefits are just benefits. 'cha-ching', as they say. It is strictly the intent of those who decreed those laws and ordered those speed bumps, their intent that we all would gain those benefits, that is to be judged as moral/immoral. And we all simply, materially benefit. And the benefits may long outlive the enactors, but you can't be moral or intend anything while you're unconscious. No consciousness, no intent. And the distinction/separation of intent and effect is still stronger! Those same people who enacted beneficial policies may have enacted other, flawed, even tragic policies, encumbering/enslaving millions, but in spite of their power, and regardless of their horrible fatal intellectual ineptitude and hubris, their acts were not immoral if/as their intents were to benefit mankind. This stands as a warning to those who emotionally cleave to righteousness, sincerity and 'purity', even simple caring etc. as necessary and sufficient grounds for trust/ action. The most sincere, loving, caring leader (and the followers) can at any time cause historical tragedy, the instant their hard, cold intellectual/scientific understandings of the situation are weaker than the power they wield.

Voluntary - It is not moral, whatever the benefit, if the act or path taken is forced or unavoidable. Again, the benefit to society may certainly accrue, but in this case the intent of the current actor is irrelevant, most likely to be self-interest at best, for instance his driving well to avoid a ticket, or a collision, or even lessening traffic congestion because his car is broken down. Forced or involuntary 'giving' is oxymoronic.

Personal sacrifice - It is not worthy of the label 'moral' if the act/gift is effortless for the actor. It is not real giving. For instance it does not rise to morality to give other peoples' money to the poor, or to give someone something you don't value.

'Equal or lower relevant fortune' - I include this bit of technicality because I would have morality to be democratic, egalitarian, 'leveling'. Voluntary 'donating up', for instance: 'so the Exalted Leader can have his 30th Rolls Royce for his 30th anniversary' would not qualify in my definition as a moral act.

And an intent/act absolutely does not need to be moral in order to be a social good! There is a vast and important field of social utility/benefit achieved as a side-effect of the teeming economic throng of private parties involved in simple economic quid pro quo transactions, motivated by personal self-interest. These are real taken opportunities for real economic wealth creation, enabled by the trust among members of a society. For those who have little taste for economics, I promise to describe later how these deals are *not* zero-sum where one must lose in order for another to gain. I will describe how real new wealth is produced by simple trading... Amoral, but still hugely socially beneficial.

We might consider the participants decision to trust the other as perhaps moral, but diminishingly so for two reasons. The first is that each actor's reward is usually contractual and immediate, and the trust is most often backed by real legal recourse if breached. Without recourse, the reach, frequency, and success of trust is minuscule. I would say that it is the intent of those that create and manage the society's legal system of fair recourse that deserves the moral label. It is they who provide the support that allows the economic activity that makes our lives better. This is a tenet of traditional conservative principals. Again, for those who have no taste for economics/business, I promise to lay out how the generic idea of business, which some may react to as hugely ugly, is nevertheless not thereby convictable as bad/immoral. How it may be pursued may at times can be both ugly and immoral, but in bulk, 'business' can and does deliver immense social benefit, even though it is amoral.

We should be well cognizant of our blessings, that we can punch a few buttons on our phone and get someone to deliver us a pizza, or someone in Thailand to send us goods he/she has spent a month creating. Morally, however, it is safest to label giving as moral when the expected benefit is utterly diffuse and unpredictable if any, except for (and ideally limited to) the immediate self-reward the actor attains for themselves in the anticipation/observation/appreciation of the benefit to the direct recipients/beneficiaries of the act. It is the empathy that makes for morality.

It is important to emphasize more about what morality is not. Obedience is *much* the lesser than morality. Obedience can be fully explained by the perceived carrots and sticks that accrue depending on the path/act options. No matter how gilt, festooned and revered the followed path is, unless the follower can cull the carrots and sticks from his reasoning, however good and valuable they may be, and be able to articulate a sufficiently personally motivating aesthetic reason for the path, the obedience is just 'playing the game' profitably. And that is not inherently bad, but it is simpler self-interest, not morality. And the remaining aesthetic reason, in order that it be moral, has to be owned and averred independently by the actor. No one else's values/aesthetics can be cited. There is no aesthetic/moral safety in blindly trusting a 'brand'. That stupidly expensive handbag can still be ugly even if it's 'from Gucci'. Blind obedience bears all the serious risk of 'just following orders'. For those who come from a reliance/trust in obedience, I can offer that obedience is saved when it becomes emancipated, becoming your dancing independently to the same music, solely for your personal joy, to your own beat.

It is important to throw in a serious warning to the devoted sincere aesthetes, those who resonate well with owning their loves, heeding their core personal empathies as motivations: Sincerity is not enough. Notice above that I was precise in attaching the judgment of moral/immoral/amoral to the *intent*. Note also that I distinguished that from the actual results, such that for instance society might well benefit from an unintentional (and therefore amoral) act. There is a serious darker side of this for the truly sincere to heed, the passionate aesthetes. The amount of disastrous social damage, waste, death and destruction that can and has been generated by the acts of powerful, ambitious, and *deeply, sincerely caring* leaders, when their ambition and care outstripped their intellectual capability to grasp the wide-ranging effects of their acts, and more importantly exceeding their grasp how much they could sadly not do, regardless of the heart-rending desire, is likely to be historically tabulated as greater loss to humanity historically than all the acts of outright malevolence.

Beware the confident. It has been shown that human self-confidence peaks long before actual intellectual capability does. The middling intelligent-and-confident will sally forth with grand plans for solutions that the fewer, smarter, and more cautious and less leader-like will know to be beyond reliable success.

"But look at all this heartbreak! We *have* to do something!"... No (and this is maybe political suicide to say), no, we don't have to do something sometimes, dismally but correctly understanding that the likelihood of waste and failure, and the attendant lessening of other attainable good, is too much higher than the emotionally promising but technically foolish foray into some heart-felt knee-jerk (heart-jerk?) acts and policies.

Aesthetics, as crucial as they are, are double-edged, ultimately 'philosophically neutral' as is everything else, a risk as well as an ally, a tool... (No easy answers) The more intense the aesthetic, the more distorting it is of perspective. Beware of the unfettered aesthetes. They will increasingly not tolerate exceptions in reality and will act with extreme prejudice to attack what is simple ugliness according to their commanding aesthetic. They will assay to make *Art* of reality, and will suffer or impart much damage to freedom and their own logical coherency to foster their big vision. Again, art is not innocent. Aesthetics are subjective *and* variable, so beware the artist you don't admire. They will not admire you either, and are more likely to act on that alone. And again, like above, beware the artist you like! If he/she ever gets their hands on social/political power, they may attempt to 'paint a global economic system' that will leave us all with only pretty oil paint to eat. I believe Venezuela's collapse is because the socialist leaders *were* sincere, with a core love and ambitious concern for the poor, and that the poor masses quite understandably trusted and followed those leaders. But because of a collective ignorance and aesthetic distrust of dismal economics and 'rich businesses', the resulting government policies crushed economic production and to the poor it gave way past 'till it hurt', serving up all the seed corn for the hungry now, never considering the tradeoff/takeaways from just the next generation...

I want to re-emphasize and make clear that the basis of morality is aesthetics. Logic has no sway except as a tool, once the basic aesthetic weights/values are simply perceived/declared/assumed. Only then can logic build the equations and scales of justice to weigh policies and agendas. In cases of moral conflict, the two sides, especially the over-simple partisans who think they are 'objectively correct', will talk past their counterparts on the other side, making logical arguments which the other side cares nothing for, because the core issue is that the two sides love/value different things, in different proportions. No scale of justice will bring two sides together when one side equates men and women while the other side knows that a woman is worth 3/5ths of a man, or one side values a zygote exactly as an infant in the crib while the other side considers that packet of undifferentiated cells with a comparative disregard as to a zit.

The noble process to grow consensus and to unite the two camps is a *beauty contest*. This is not silly or trivial, in fact the exact opposite. It is an aesthetic contest of competing beauties in the very most serious way. For instance, the competition between modernity and historically static cultures is moved/affected more effectively by 'soft power', the relative overall attractive-nesses of life's opportunities, beauties and powers competing in the forums of Instagram, Facebook, and low-brow TV series than by any competing political pronouncements and initiatives from leaders.

Here is a test of the 'morality is based on aesthetics' claim. Please take any morality position you choose. Select any one particular tenet, such as 'thou shalt not steal', or any you may make up. For it to meet my definition, it will be fully expressed/expressible as a statement "It is <good xor bad> to <insert active verb and con-ditions here>". 'Xor' means exclusively one or other, never both nor neither. Now imagine a visiting Martian asking you why that thing is bad/good. Cite your reasons fully, as if to a child, and now imagine a follow-up about the basis for the reasons you gave. "You said abc is bad, and when I asked why, you said it is because abc causes xyz. Why is xyz bad?". Iterate this process once or twice more, and very shortly you will come (I assert) to a very basic, unquestionable-to-you base reason, such as 'infant deaths are bad', or 'freedom is good', or 'God is good'. Now please face your frustration if this innocent skeptic asks you one more time to answer why that seemingly obvious final thing is good/ bad. I assert that here you have arrived at your set of "duh", "it's obvious", "I can't/won't question that", "Someone must be bad, a communist etc. to question that" value statements, *purely aesthetic stands*, that are the foundation of your morality. You should be aware of them and own them as your core personal *aesthetics*.

Note that for most such moral tenets, there is a quickly reached, simple and shared level at which most normal humans would have said "well sure, duh?' to the reason *but nevertheless without articulating any further reason/basis*, just implying that the reason/value was obvious. I submit that these are purely aesthetic opinions of the believer, as unquestioned as whether they are hungry when they are, bored when they are etc. These are the unquestioned loves/hates made/felt pre-logic. This is not to say that morality is vacuous, or that its subjectivity makes it useless. You have a right to your deepest-felt cares, loves and allegiances, and you should have the moral courage to uphold and defend them *because they represent your *feelings*. And the commonality of many of these aesthetic positions across societies is based, not on any 'objectivity', but rather because of the commonality of subjective social identities (the 'bigger selves') held by/among all the people and other beings, in their societies. There are plenty of examples of clear moral opinion and 'big self' sacrificial action by social animals.

And note the necessarily personal, individual authority that this requires from you, for your moral stand. There is no deferring to any external authority allowed/possible. The 'why' questions do not stop until you are the direct answerer. The question is why you believe, trust, or agree with anything anyone else says, real or imagined. God is no escape, because first and always, you judge God, according to your personal private reasons/aesthetics. Gods are no leaders except by your explicit leave. You are ever still responsible, and solely so, for your choices. You are utterly and always the author of your morality, no matter what boiler-plate you accrete to yourself, that is your private act, according to your own and sole values. It remains for you to collect and own the moral position/value statements that you personally and independently aver as your stands. It is what and who *you* personally and individually love. Remember, obedience must be supported personally, ultimately aesthetically according you your own *personal* values, else it's just following orders, and relegates the follower to much less than moral, much less than full self-aware consciousness.

Absolutely use/let logic be applied to your thoughts and actions in support of your loves. Absolutely use logic and experience to grow and consider these, your usually unquestioned loves, as they are *your* opinions, and you may rightly find they merit expansion, generalization or substantial correction as you your-self grow and change and learn. For instance we (most) all hope a persons' love for children quickly or at least eventually reaches a clear generalization that it does not matter the color of their skin. We (mostly) hope that those who start out fearing/hating people just because they like the cultural norms they grew up in, that seem opposite to what 'we' like, will narrow their disagreement to a tenet-by-tenet basis, not persecuting the 'others' en masse. So, yes, morality is affected by nurture and nature, and is malleable. It is *not* inherently resolvable to one 'objective'(in the colloquial sense, like the rules of chess) platform. When there is conflict, as there will always be in a world of conscious individuals with the temerity to hold their own aesthetic reactions/decisions, the positive resolution is approached, to the degree there can be any movement, by the outcome of that continuing beauty contest, that utmost serious set of choices we make for what we want out of life for us and ours.

Your morality represents *you*, your greater self, you affirmatively including and holding all and who you love. You are the creator, author and curator of your greater self.

Chapter 7

On selflessness and selfishness...

As we linger in, and ponder this perspective of the axiomatic self, there may be a whiff of 'social guilt', a resistance, a preference for selflessness over self-centeredness and a loathing of selfishness. We can absolutely fix this. :)

I would like you to consider the assertion that selfishness does not exist, except when there is an aggrieved party who was cheated or unfairly disadvantaged by the selfish act. If a solitary starving man in the wilderness somehow comes across a long-deserted cache of sustenance, it is not selfishness of them to eat his/her fill, more, and take all he can carry. It is only if we imagine/posit that there are some other starving people nearby that this starving man should know about and consider, and share with, that we could now consider them selfish to take it all. If this starver was travelling with his family, it would of course be selfish not to share with them. Sharing equally among the family would seen as the moral (non-selfish) act. But now extend the story to a known second family soon to show up. What was a moral sharing a second ago is now selfish from the perspective of the two families as the relevant stakeholders, the new 'relevant/operant society'. But if this cache of food was perishable, and would spoil before the second family could arrive, they would revert to irrelevancy and sharing among the first family would be fine.

This story of increasing stakeholders is about your greater self. Let's end this story with the two families being the full set of practical stakeholders, the appropriate bigger social self you would adopt in order to define morality at the time, for the circumstances. *You* would care, love, and act in equal consideration of all them, you would temporarily think and subjectively feel/*be* this greater self emotionally. And you would *not* be being 'selfless'. Presumably you would eat and drink your share. It is just that the 'self' you chose to care for was, at that time, a society of two families. Even if you did not feed yourself, for whatever sacrificial reason, the 'self' you adopted for your allotting food would be those you did choose to feed. So selflessness is actually meaningless as I define it. What generates morality is the *bigger* self, specifically the social self you adopt by considering who you will/can care for, as you would for your individual self. Immorality comes from making decisions that favor one subset of society over another equally-deserving/needing one. Our job is then to understand the effects of our actions, and consider them in the light of all the people they effect. No selflessness, rather the opposite, being as *big* a self as needed, so that no one external can reasonably say you/we were selfish. And this bigness need only reach the practical stakeholders for the current issue. It was never a moral issue whether you ate or wasted your casserole when mom told you that there were kids starving in Europe...

My personal stand is that life, all life, anywhere is what I identify with, admittedly in varying and biased degrees. Life as a whole is my 'biggest self'. I will absolutely declare my distinct and unapologetic bias for humans over mosquitoes etc. This stand describes my core aesthetic base for my morality. As such, I openly ponder and plot the full exploitation of every single resource on the planet in order that we sustain most all life (sorry polio), especially human life, as absolutely sustainably as possible on Earth, and even generate a diaspora to some other planets if we can find some. If we can find anyone to feel shorted by this, than I accept that I am selfish in exactly this way... ;) See chapter 11 for more on self interest, 'selfishness'

Chapter 8

The Enormity and Beauty of the Subjective Realm

I want to do more to remove the Western prejudice/taint given to the 'subjective'. Your subjective space is not some cloistered little nook in your psyche where you store your biases and embarrassments. It is the sum of your entire consciousness, and the field in which anything new you may know will reside. Again,

> Subjective - Any thing that depends on a mind/consciousness in order for that thing to exist.

The Western negative colloquial connotations for 'subjective' are 'capricious', 'influenced by personal feelings, tastes, or opinions'. By my definition, these pejoratives are clearly not indicated. Yes, the subjective is 'influenced by the personal', it *is* the personal, intimately associated with and the private product of the individual. But all in subjectivity need not be capricious. The subjective is in fact rich with utterly reliable and invariant entities, universal truths.

Logic - The discipline of coherent thought

This is my definition of logic. Mathematics is a subset of it. Thought requires a thinker. Mathematics is subjective! And this is not to say it is variable in its products. The assertion/calculation that 2 + 2 = 4 is subjective and *mind-invariant*. It is freely and identically inferable/derivable by any mind that shall manifest sufficient logical coherence.

Note well that mathematics is mind-invariant, *not* mind-independent. It nevertheless depends on the mind in order to exist. Mathematics is a rich discipline/algorithm for thinkers to generate universal, mind invariant truths, those truths that shall be identical in all minds that coherently perceive them.

None of this is objective in my parlance. There are no '2's or '+'s drifting around in the physical universe, waiting to be absorbed into brains when sentient life emerged.

And yes, we absolutely and profitably rely of mathematics in forming our predictions and formulae in physics. But this is not to impute physicality or objectivity (as I define it) to mathematics/logic. The reason we find the value and congruence between our logic/math and our modelling of the physical world is because the coherency of our logic finds a harmony with the apparent and totally independent coherence of the universe itself. If instead the universe was not the 'global closed system' of physics, the encompassing of all causality, but instead was perhaps a grand, dramatic soap opera narrative of some fulminating celestial auteur, then just like our regular soap operas, no matter how pristine the coherency of our logic, our calculations would be bootless to predict the next twist in the plot. And indeed when we apply our calculations to the systems we posit, and when the results differ from our calculations, we always find that there is/ was some aspect of physical reality that we did not include, so the system we posited was not coherent/closed.

The distinction between mind-invariant and mind-independent is important. The latter term is used often in philosophical arguments to hand-wavedly, hopefully-but-falsely bridge the subjective/objective separation. 'Mind independent' = 'objective' in my terms, and nothing in the mind is mind independent. Everything in the mind is mind dependent, subjective, and some of this subjectivity is more reliable and provable than anything in physics. This is an example of why the proximity of subjectivity is much less a field requiring doubt than the objective realm. I will show later that the very ethos and aesthetics suitable to philosophy will differ depending on whether the pursuit is in the subjective or objective realm.

And all beauty, all horror, all meaning reside completely and only in the mind. Beauty and horror are your aesthetic judgments of ideas and circumstances. Beauty and meaning are not intrinsic to objects, they are applied to objects in the context of the judging, symbolizing mind. All classification and all generalization of objects/reality are acts of your mind. Consider any two objects.

By simple linguistic and logical consistency the two objects are utterly separate and distinct. If we should want to compare these two objects, and perhaps generalize them as 'the same sort of thing', it is we who parse the objects into aspects/characteristics/attributes, and then choose our operant list of characteristics that must match in order to define similarity. Similarity is not intrinsic to objects. They exist independently and objectively share *nothing*. it is only the applique of set membership that we confer on them in our mind that/where they 'share' anything.

There will be more on meaning, but briefly, meaning is a narrative/image that we associate, for brevity as a mnemonic, to an object we create/co-opt as a symbol. The successful transfer of meaning, even if only to oneself, is when we remember and re-feel/re-see the payload (that rich narrative/feeling) while considering the object we importuned as the symbol. Meaning is an act of mind, a utilitarian shorthand for encoding, remembering, and linking ideas. By/as itself the entire objective/physical world just *is*. It is intrinsically devoid of, and independent of meaning, a purely subjective behavior. It is we who apply/imagine meaning to the moon... if only that we remember what we thought the next time we consider the moon. See chapter 11 for more on meaning.

Chapter 9

A first quick visit to the objective realm, the universe of physics

The Universe, my operant definition - The totality of physical space-time, enclosing/requiring all relevant causality for anything within the universe. The 'global closed system' of physics

If we wish to understand everything in the universe, we have no option but to include/find everything relevant. Specifically, if we declare/surmise that some thing is relevant to some aspect/element of the universe, then that thing must be part of the universe, symmetrically affected by anything it affects.

To an acceptable engineering/practical degree of accuracy for simple problems, in physics we define a 'local closed system' to include all the relevant-to-the-desired-degree-of-accuracy causes and effects. For instance, to calculate the trajectory of a thrown rock, we can make simple calculations which for instance, may not need to practically consider (1) the frictional effects of air or wind, and certainly do not need to consider/include (2) the movement of the earth, but if we increase the accuracy needs or scale of the problem, such as if we now want to plot the trajectory for the current longest-range military projectiles then fascinatingly, we need to consider all of those (1) and (2)!

In any experiment, if we apply exact logic/math to our assumed set of relevancies, and yet the observed results are different than what we calculate, then, after rechecking our logic, we must then find what else there is, what unknown or unconsidered influences within the universe are afoot that swayed the results.

This definition of the universe is not to say we know all that is in the universe. It is to say that the only rightful bound of the universe is the all-relevancy-encompassing one that makes the universe coherent to and within itself, so that it is amenable to modelling by coherent thought. And we may never know all the aspects of the universe that materially contribute to the observations we make. It is just to say that we will yet consider that the unknowns are nevertheless, by definition and rationality, part of the universe.

A distinctly powerful aspect of this definition emerges, for use in apologetics. As above, anything that is relevant to the universe is *in* the universe, **by definition**. If there is or was anything to be labeled 'God' that is considered to be or was instrumental/

relevant to the objective realm or anything in the universe as so defined, then that God is or was **part of, in the universe**, and classified as objective in my parlance. When/if such a God is ever logically defined, it will be inexorably in the wheel-house of physics, amenable and subject to the logic of physical calculations, and by symmetry of cause and effect in the universe, this God is/was affected/changed, in equal degree by anything he/she/it/they affected. Nothing ever escapes or enters the universe, no information, no light, no energy. Thus there is no time or external perspective where a universe as a whole is at all detectable or relevant.

From the objective perspective, if there are any things other than what is in the physical universe, then those things are at best hypotheses, such as when the subjective realm is allowed, as a never well-defined conjecture. We actually see only behavior, not thought, not feelings as such. And symmetrically, from the subjective perspective, as per Solipsism, if there is anything in the objective set (the universe), it is at best a hypothesis by those who take on faith that the universe really exists. From either side, the other is optional, entertained or denied at will, directly unaffecting and unaffected by the other.

As grist for another chapter, I suggest that theists reading this book, and wanting to integrate God into this ontology will find that putting God into the subjective category (and recall that by definition it can exclusively be one or the other) will have God deliver most of their desired benefits. God is certainly a central, and reliably productive/helpful concept in the ontology of the minds of millions. For those fewer among them whose philo-sophical pursuits make it interesting to integrate God with ontol-ogies like this, I suggest considering God as like a principle in a calculus for generating answers to certain important questions, and like other ontologies, good for answering some sorts of questions, and less so for other types. God will never be a decid-ing factor in any physics calculation. Render unto physics that which is physics'. Use God as centrally intended, in questions of 'ought'. Perhaps in another chapter we can work on a trans-form function, a formula for translating between a God-based calculus of 'ought' and the identity-and-aesthetics-based moral calculus+art that I present in this book. Just like whether one chooses a Cartesian coordinate geometry or a Polar coordinate one, what matters is whether we come to the same answers. And where we come to different answers, we can examine the social world to triangulate and judge the relative predictive power of the two algorithms.

ABOUT TIME...

Take any physics equation and solve for time. You will see it is a measure of change. Without time, there is no change, and sym-metrically, without change there is no time! Imagine any circum-stance where nothing changes. Time is then meaningless unless you introduce/add a running clock to the picture, or you add some other external changing aspects to the picture to deliver change, which then can meter/exhibit time, to then be able to say that 'nothing changed within that circumstance for some duration, defined by the changing clock or during the changes in those added changing externalities.

Note that time, space, energy and matter are not independent, they are bound and interdependent, expressible only in each others terms. The universe *delivers and includes* all relevant space, time, matter and energy. The universe is not some bubble to be observed from without. Remember, no light, no information, no energy, nothing goes into or out of the universe. It has zero external presence. Specifically, there was no 'la-de-da' external time and space where some impossible observer could be seeing nothing, then "poof, there's a universe! How did that happen?". Apologists sometimes come to an important logical need for something uncaused. Causality is, in important part a temporal relationship. Because the universe *delivers* all real time, the universe itself, as a whole, is unchanging (in fact undetectable and moot!) from without, and is a-priori and *uncaused* as a whole, with respect to anything in it. All time, all change is intra-universe. Defined as such, this universe will (fully-and-only) fill that logical need.

And there is a desire to avoid 'infinite regression'. There can be a beginning of time, without contradiction to the above. Consider entropy, as plotted by the second law of thermodynamics in physics. We observe and prove by the mathematics of probability that with the flow of time, entropy (the degree of complexity/possibilities/chaos/disorder) inexorably increases globally (in the universe overall). There absolutely are local places and conditions within the universe where, with the regular deliverance of energy to a local system which causes harmonics and by which stability and order is retained, even increased, at the cost of the discharge of the low-energy sacrificial byproducts out of the local system. The temporary and salutary conditions and relationship of the Earth and Sun, so as to support life, is an example. For as long as the fortuitous external energy situation lasts, this sort of local humming environment, if it plays for enough billions of years, is suitable for biogenesis, a more delicate, complex and fortuitous but-then-self-reinforcing rhythm of identity that can 'play off/exploit' a water cycle and carbon cycle etc. In other words, life forms themselves are examples of entropy-defeating identity-maintaining cyclic systems that persist/maintain by tapping provided external energy and exuding the by-products into the greater 'outdoors'. But universe-wide entropy increases with time.

Now consider/imagine time in reverse and the universe thereby has inexorably less entropy/complexity/chaos/possibilities. Things/states become ever simpler and orderly. Possibilities diminish. I assert that this mental exercise reaches a mathematical/logical minimum/terminus!

Let us declare a simple numeric measure of complexity, a quantification, perhaps crudely expressed as 'the Number Of Possible States'. Simply taking this retrograde extrapolation to the limit must reach the NOPS of one, where it can get no simpler! The very beginning of time reaches what must be a simplest *changing* state, where complexity increases from none (NOPS/all is one) to the next simplest, two, with a cataclysmic split. Each of these 'states' thence sub-splitting and so on. Note that time/ change requires relativity, which requires a minimum complexity of two. Thus time, and the universe began with a split from one to two.

To those of us avid technical philosophers and scientists who want nailed-down clarity and details, this description is unattractively detail-less, redolently 'loose', sadly yin-yangy, artsy and interpretive. I assert and will show that it *has to be*, that it cannot have more detail! These two initial 'things/states' that split from an even simpler one, are *necessarily* devoid of any richness of triangulatable/corroborable detail or qualities. They simply and logically *must* lack any complexity that would provide any more of a logical/descriptive handle on them such that they would be amenable to more complex consideration.

This beginning of time will bear no detail, and our trying to add any color or character to these entities will be fatal to the truth. I assert that some very real states/things are *just too simple* for humanly articulable conception/expression. It may be that our facility for language and thought has a lower limit to its grasp, defined by a minimum degree of complexity of the subject matter. I suspect that we are already seeing the effects of this in our efforts to understand quantum mechanics, where as we focus on increasingly smaller-and-necessarily-simpler objects, the objects are too simple to reliably coherently bear the richer connotations we want to infer when we call them 'particles' and/or 'waves'.

Again, there is no time when there is no change. So that 'all is one' state existed for no time. Nothing would matter if you pretended to be an observer watching within this latent universe staying 'all together as one', for an instant or for half an eternity. That instant and that 'half an eternity' are equal and moot, undefinable, just like in the subjective space, if you are in a sensory isolation chamber, then sleep then wake up, or did you sleep? Maybe you just shut your eyes for an instant? Was there any time? Again, you have to introduce a clock or other change in order to manifest time.

Objective time and the universe started with the kinetic, that first split. The universe has existed for all real time. For those that ask for a cause for the split, I can only offer a hand-wave that it is in the 'inherent instability of oneness', but I must point out again our conceptual limits, and that the actual unsurpassed simplicity of this early universe cannot offer/bear true descriptions with any humanly satisfying, inference-rich, pithy concrete answers that would functionally relate to practical calculations of today.

ON THE NATURAL AND SUPERNATURAL

I would say that anything and everything in the universe, known or as yet unknown, by the above definition, is integral and necessary to the completion of the universe, and there is utterly no logical reason, no 'non-drama-desiring' reason all of it should be deemed as other than natural. The term 'supernatural' seems to be a precipitate and self-anointing imperious colloquiality, as if we have the authority and 'higher wisdom' to know nature, and to be able to deem what belongs to nature ('base normalcy in our view') and what should be deemed as beyond nature in some way, that there is any relevant beyond nature.

By the given definition of the universe there is no objective, relevant beyond, and in the subjective realm, it is you who generates/perceives all reality. You and your every imagination are natural. Nature = reality. Supernatural is an lax ontological category for free-form 'explanations' using 'relaxed-fit logic', for anything as yet unexplained naturally, whether by unknowingly incomplete effort or by a determined desire/need that it not be explained naturally (ruins the story line). It is a pressure relief valve for those who want/need answers dearly enough that correctness is secondary, and for those with powerful desires/needs to not accept nature/reality as it is, as everything. In some times and cultures and mindsets, this is a valuable, even saving approach, allowing a reliably optimistic motivating narrative.

Chapter 10

More on you, your spectrum of self

I have covered isolating/locating you in your subjective space, and distinguishing you logically from the faculties you have. For instance, inexplicably (from a purely subjective perspective) you do seem armed with facilities like memory you can traverse and relive, etc, but you are not your memories. You have the aesthetic ability to judge, to apply a good/bad value to an idea or memory. You are the judger, but you are not the judgements, and you are not the things you judge. You are not the ideas or experiences. Reduced ultimately, you are simply the occupant of your subjective point of view in your subjective space. Logically and philosophically this is important to isolate/distinguish you as the 'necessary being' before all else in your proximal subjective reality. This is Zen-like, pacifying, achieving maximal isolation/

separation/perspective. But this is not a sure-and-permanent safe haven.

There are times when such a stance is (from an objective perspective) dangerous and that the opposite stance is apt/necessary, that you should be fully attached, fully engaged, 'in the zone', acting and reacting with full and instant energy bound to the pursuit of your set agenda and your whole, greatest, 'inclusive' self.

Practically, what use or value are you, even just to yourself, without these faculties and the strength of your commitments and attachments? If, for instance, you had/have no memory, you would still be that enduring center of your experience/subjectivity, but you will never realize it. For one, memory is crucial to your awareness of your enduring self as the ongoing commonality and as the enduring unique recipient of your experiences. You need memory just to experience time/change, to be able to store an image of reality so that you can later compare it to the current state, to detect a change. It is indeed a deep and sad loss to watch someone's self diminish as their memory, and thus ultimately the very ability to experience time, is eroded out from under them by Alzheimer's.

Aesthetics is another cruciality. There have been cases where otherwise fully sentient and healthy people have suffered damages that separated them exactly and specifically from their own aesthetic reactivity, and are deeply depressed that life goes on, but nothing has meaning (value), no motivation anywhere. So, let's now rather look more at our greater self, including all our faculties and what we have constructed, asserted, owned, and loved etc.

From a practical motivational behavioral perspective, you are what you love, that your identity is the collection of what you identify with, what you care about. Yes, to love is to identify with. To this degree, you define yourself. And yes, this spans the spectrum of your core unchanging values, to your instant-to-instant aesthetic reactions, conscious or subconscious. For the moment I am ignoring how you are defined by your capability aspects, those powers you have to detect and react to stimuli, which are a typically stable set of tools for you, which in a bigger picture may distinguish and 'identify' you, such as if you have particularly excellent hearing, or taste, or if you are preternaturally focused and expert in auditory input because you are blind, etc. If you do have some particular excellence, you may consciously identify with that, and thereby (consciously or unconsciously) alter or bias your motivations/identity/behavior to exploit it or even change your view of the world to project your personal skills as more important. The Cuban cigar-maker whose product is good enough to be imported by presidents will likely put themself and his skills as closer to the successful execution of political power and status than anyone else would consider... Trump's hair stylist may be right in that regard! There are cases where a person may have clear and distinctive attributes or qualities, but for some reason the person does not love/identify with them, and for these people, their interests and pursued/expressed identity may not involve those attributes, which may lie fallow, or worse.

For now I am focusing only on the motivational inputs, and specifically your good/bad evaluation of them, that govern when and whether you take up any of your tools to do anything in the first place. At the lower, more stable levels of this spectrum, I place those motivations/identity elements for which you have much less freedom/power or desire to choose/alter your choice/values/ identity. Like the base of a pyramid, down to the epigenetics, to the DNA. For instance, you would be motivated strongly and reliably (usually, by default) toward biologically favorable environments, brooking only notable and specific exceptions such as people climbing Everest etc. being decidedly temporary and strongly effortful in their high-level conscious committed motivations to clearly ideated values. Such exceptions actually demonstrate our freedom of choice/identity/values (and their limits) because they often require committed abrogations of important, normal and low-level, usually stable values, such as the desires for physical comfort and safety. One class of the most extreme examples of conscious choices of identity overriding our common lower base values is in those who decide to die for social/political causes.

Here is an example of how one of our more basic, less mutable identity parameters could be consciously chosen and altered: If we as a species (the social inclusive 'I'), collectively in each of our consensual social selves, for some odd aesthetic/political reason, decided that a given skin color was the best, we could collectively take only a few generations of our coordinated individual efforts (united in our shared social identity), make purposeful, selective breeding choices to change and manifest this choice of otherwise significantly stable attribute of identity. First though, I want to describe how you, your operant identity, can change materially, moment to moment.

At your most evanescent level of identity, you are exaggeratedly (though not solely) what you are consciously paying attention to. When I say 'you are', I mean what you are behaviorally, internally reactively, predictably to what you are attending. For instance, you might be engaged in a story where you are at first attracted to favor one character as a protagonist, and later easily shift your allegiance to another. Or you could be engaged in a game where coins are tossed, and you get points for every head, and then later it shifts to every tail. In either of these changing scenarios, with or without your further conscious consideration of the value structure, while your focused/defined motivation does not change, however trivial it may be in the larger context of life, to the degree you do focus on the head/tails events, or the revealed characters and fates of the fictional characters, simple B.F. Skinner tests and lie-detector galvanic skin reactions will all demonstrate that you will react physically, instant-to-instant as the story, or the otherwise stultifyingly boring series of heads and tails unfolds.

To the degree you focus, ie: to the degree you choose to identify with these events of the moment, that is who you are, viscerally. Of course at this most 'volatile' short-term re-writeable level, your consciousness and subconsciousness may easily and instantly have competitors for your attention, potentially switching 'who you are', what you react to, and in the case of the conscious level, focus on. The phone may ring from your spouse, or you may subconsciously detect and react to changes in the periphery, like the room becoming hotter, causing you to shift your position, or delude yourself that for some reason your sweater has suddenly become itchy, so you distractedly take it off while trying to stay focused on the story plot or count of tails, etc. The point is that at this level you have maximal freedom/instability, consciously and subconsciously, in what your values/motivations are, your operant identity.

These coin-toss-level values are most easily variable because they are simple, standalone evaluations, not connected to any other of your existing values. A step lower (more stable) in the spectrum are your chosen values that derive from or support/connect to other of your values, in a system, such as your favoring sunny days because you're a competitive tanner, but who would wistfully and begrudgingly accept that an occasionally rainy day is necessary for the farmers and planet, and therefore good in the big-boy sense, but still not like them in the easier, narrower 'me me me' sense... More seriously though, your identity/values in life are decidedly not standalone. They are derived and enmeshed in the entire warp and weft of your world view/ontology, the plan through which you choose to see, navigate, and manipulate reality for the promulgating of your agenda, from food and shelter to social power and standing. This level of your chosen identity is much more rigid, and though changeable in principal, takes concerted and rare conscious commitment and risk in accepting or even considering the new, when the ramifications threaten to pull an ugly long run in the fabric of your world-view as currently woven, whose status quo may have suited and succeeded for all of life till now.

Some people who have for instance been initially and deeply inculcated in some racial or dogmatic religious belief systems may nevertheless later come to some equally deep and changing convictions that cause them to renounce and replace large swaths of their world view. It is doable, but there must be deeply found reasons and a perception of significant new psychological benefits to be gained in doing so. This is a rare occurrence. To generalize from Sinclair:

"It is very difficult to get someone to understand something when their livelihood, social status or long-held values depend on them not understanding it."

In a serious moderated by-invite forum on logic, philosophy and religion, I have witnessed highly intelligent people engaged in exacting debate, who when pushed to the limit have explicitly been willing to renounce logic itself, rather than accept/admit to a flaw in their expressed world view that would, if faced, require significant unraveling their base ontology. And this was independent of, and in the absence of any practical differences in our derived social policies and values. We each would want and do the same things in practical terms for ourselves, our neighbors, and our society. For the most part we would be ideal mutual neighbors. The only difference was conceptual, that we differed starkly in the model/rationale from which we arrived at the same moral social answers! And this is to focus this book on its narrow philosophical purpose of logical coherence. In the real world, to the degree we can rely on our neighbors for the practical social behaviors and motivating values, we should concentrate on being happy, not needing that they be logically coherent as to their rationalizations.

Chapter 11

Your greater self.
Selfishness exonerated?

I have spent much of my typing till now enabling/encouraging/ requiring you to logically distinguish you, at the center of your consciousness, from your attachments, faculties and desires, pains and troubles, chosen group identities etc. I have been highlighting and isolating you at your center, temporarily minimizing and focusing you to/at your real subjective core, the resident of the geometric point of view at the center of your subjectivity.

This process is intellectually clarifying, to know yourself and to be able to distinguish and then own and manage the specific attachments/identifications you are now able to be more consciously aware of. And this conscious self-awareness is crucial, because these loves, identifications, attachments will sway your behavior whether you know them or not. To *be*, as a stand-alone consciousness, to have freedom from unconscious influence requires you know, justify and own the influences you accept. And lastly, it is key that you understand that it is you who, once aware, affirmatively make/keep these attachments. To the degree that you want to actively *be* as a consciousness, you define yourself, self-aware, self-defining. Nothing out there grabs your psyche and glues itself to your identity. With consciousness you become the curator and author of your identity, your values.

However, from a practical life-pursuit perspective it is exactly unmotivating to consider yourself, apart from your values, your motivators. I am not saying that the Zen-like state is of no use or beauty. It absolutely has some attraction and utility, particularly in an era or life circumstance where there is much to be troubled about and little practical means of understanding or changing the circumstances. Mental peace is restful.

But as soon as you choose to get off the meditation couch and re-occupy all your loves and cares, this denatured Zen place can sometimes be exposed as having been a dangerous retreat and delay, a waste of objective time that (if you have the means) could have instead been spent acting and producing in your interests, like accepting the lure of sleep when marching out of the snow seems too hard.

Rest assured that your loves and concerns are in no way trivial or condemnable just because they are (at least now, if my typing has been clear) understood by you as intellectually detachable and arguably voluntary. Your attachments are your source of joy and feedback. They and their fates are a crucial sounding board for you in your judging your constructed world view, and in verifying the 'greater you' (to be defined).

To be fair and clear, in keeping with 'no easy answers', this other direction, the maximizing of self by the affirmation and inclusion of your loves and attachments as/in yourself is no less a double-edged sword than the self-minimizing escape/detachment mode. All avenues that would deliver you pain and loss are exactly and logically symmetrically the result of attachment to your joys and hopes. Every love/attachment/identification you make with any externality at all, is an exposure, a ligature, equally to uplift or pull down, and always a drop in freedom as much as a drop in insecurity, always an increment of bondage as much as an increase in bonding.

In my typing I cannot offer a permanent balm or safe haven for anyone, any natural mind like my own. The best I can offer is that you develop a tactical fluency so you can most ably, clearly, self-honestly choose/identify when you should gird yourself with the courage and enterprise to change what you can and should, including (and because of) your operant identity (attachments), and alternately the power to manifest and benefit from grace when you can't/shouldn't act or change your identity, your attachments. Fundamentally love/attachment is a *bet*, a logically symmetrical risk/reward condition. So, symmetrically is detachment. Attachment increases stability, allows for communion/influence and decreases freedom. Symmetrically, detachment increases freedom and isolation, and decreases stability.

And there will most often never be the necessary information to guarantee either choice as correct in a given context. No easy answers, and we don't know the future. In the face of insecurity however, the psychological benefit of 'known future' narratives is historically obvious.

So, hoping I have established the general 'philosophical neutrality' of attachments, that they are not inherently unalloyed goods or bads, but rather hopeful commitments, we have a question: Is there a way we can pursue life reliably 'profitably' (from the Bhutanese Gross National Happiness perspective), that we are most successful in the pursuit of happiness?

I believe so, and that there should be no guilt, fear or revulsion in this goal, particularly its personal nature. Ours is an innocent and real predicament that we cannot know a right/guaranteed path, no matter what we choose.

And no guilt is yet appropriate for affirmatively trying to maximize your personal joy. Joy is not a zero-sum game.

I do understand the fear and even in some, revulsion of acknowledging conscious, personal, individual self-determination, self-identification, owning oneself. There are people whose life-feedback has conditioned them by failures or losses or culture-specific social pressures to think that they cannot/should not trust nor even assiduously consider themselves per se. Indeed today there are societies where the consideration of self is utterly dangerous because even the subconsciously generated manifestations of an individually chosen and crafted identity are a red-flag of non-conformity that constitutes an immediate target for attack. In such societies, ones personal feelings are cloistered, and most safety and status is achieved only by presenting as an exemplar/cog of the group according to your assigned role.

So, (and perhaps belatedly in this text), the warning must be given that for some of you reading this, the mere understanding of what I am saying may be dangerous for you within your culture. Is it safe, or even attractive to consider and wield yourself separately and independently, transcendent of your culture? To be, or not to be (uniquely you)? For you, this may be a clarity vs. comfort decision I suggested early. The value is that if we can individually transcend our base culture, just so far as to be able to personally own our moral choices, and personally defend or reject any of *our* culture's tenets, one by one, each on our own individual terms, then we have a hope for an operant global moral society.

I shall start simply and personally. I will describe the assembly that is my larger self. First and foremost, I identify with my spouse and children, and then my greater family. My attachment to them is absolute to the depth of my strength and courage, and 'aesthetically axiomatic' so I find it natural and subconsciously motivated/satisfying for me to react positively to, and to enjoyingly consider things that accord with their interest, as much as for my own. For an illustration, on a wilderness camping trip, if I were to discover ripe patch of blackberries, I would un/prethinkingly alert my family to the find, and thence care that everyone got their share. If I instead kept the find to myself, my family (and you) could surely call me selfish. But as/when I clad myself with a 'greater self' including those I love that I can affect, my reaction and desires include them. The operant definition of "I" has changed, and grown.

Now, was my perfect sharing unselfish? Perhaps surprisingly, initially, before I make my constructions perfectly clear, I prefer to say that I *was* selfish, though not in the pejorative tone. I was selfish as my greater self, exploiting the windfall for *our* benefit. I become a moral actor, and my greater self is a 'we', those I deem deserving of morality. And given the scenario so far, there is no one being shorted/neglected, so this operational 'selfishness', with the all-relevant-beings-inclusive self is totally beneficial.

And now a next step, added context: What if there were other campers near or foreseeable to the area who might like/get some of the berries before they rotted? Might they still say I was selfish (in the standard pejorative tone) to have kept them all to me and my family? Yes! But...

For selfishness to be a pejorative, it implies and requires a relevant and excluded/cheated group or other. If I am alone, hundreds of miles from anyone, and find some berries, and I eat them all, I am acting in my sole, most narrow-self benefit, but because/if there are no other knowable/possible relevant stakeholders, no practically slighted others, then my acting in my sole interest, as narrowly selfishly as I can be, is beneficial for me and has no pejorative taint.

If now, I recall and assert my current example of my greater self, me and my family, if there were no others near, I would say that in sharing the berries among us, I acted the same, in my own greater self-interest (selfish in the context of my operant self being 'me and my family'). Again, this 'greater selfishness' is beneficial to the operant/defined greater self, and is in no way bad if there is no one else practically disenfranchised.

The bigger the 'self' that you actually personally emotionally have/choose, the more there are who stand to benefit when you act in the interests of your chosen, operant greater self. This is the social/moral you.

Again, this 'greater selfishness' is never bad except if there are others, excluded who have really lost out by your acts. I choose to identify with all humans on the planet, indeed with all living things. I will aver to act 'selfishly' in my/our interest. I would plot and promote a calculated scheme to maximally exploit all the resources we have on earth, so as to maximize the happiness and sustainable duration of all life on earth for as long as possible. Call me 'selfish'. I am, in a big good way. I'm hoping to minimize the number of people who would object because all would be part of the 'big me' for whom I was advocating.

Have as big a self as you want/can, then be 'selfish' and they will all benefit. Just be aware to own your self, if there are others you materially exclude. They, and anyone else who considers the excluded as part of their greater self will have cause to call you narrowly selfish.

It is perhaps the biggest risk of the power of Western society that we are ever more able to materially affect people at a greater distance than the reach of our compassion, our greater self. When we had little power, the degree of morality needed for survival needed only to extend to ones family and what few neighbors one might possibly affect. Now a tweet can belittle/alienate others instantly on the other side of the planet.

Consider Mother Theresa, for a moment. (for ease, let it be the stereotype, not the complex and checkered real person described by Hitchens). Most would say she was 'selfless' in her devotion to the poor. I understand the meaning, but in my current parlance I would say that she was tireless in promoting/supporting her chosen greater self, the world's poor. She was beneficially selfish for her large constituency. Even if she starved by sharing her every meal equally bite-by-bite with every poor person in reach, she was acting for her chosen greater self, in the severely democratic proportions she would be taking. Her identity, her choice, and her accepted risks from this chosen attachment. Some people actually do discount/deny themselves from their greater self, such as if Mother Theresa would never eat a thing if there was one more needy person in reach. That could be (but wasn't) her choice, and such self-denigrating positions are self-limiting... In her position of power, it should (and was) reasonable/understood that the net gain to her constituency was better if she stayed alive and healthy, compared to the added benefit to the starving by donating her every meal. So again though, from my framework, she was tireless and self-motivated in support of her chosen society, her chosen greater self-interest.

So, now I want to list some points and ramifications of this chapter:

1. Acting in your self interest is natural.

2. Acting in your self interest is *good* for you. No shame! Goodness is not a zero-sum game!

3. Acting in your self interest is your job. No one else is logically more responsible for that.

It is necessary for your survival. You are a full-fledged card-carrying independent member of life. Neither this universe nor any society nor any logical sustainable economy is designed or should be designed or can sustainably be designed to automatically produce and spoon-feed you(us) what you/we need, let alone what you in your creative and evolving consciousness may come to want to empower you at any new moment or turn in your life. You/we survive and prosper by our successful efforts at creative *profitable* behavior, specifically the creation of wealth. Go out and look for those berries! Go out and grow those berries. Trade some berries for some of the eggs your neighbor is producing. Just *trading* creates wealth! You may love your berries, but after the sixth pint of the day, you may be sick of them, and to you those last fourteen baskets you have can rot for all you care.

Value is not intrinsic, it is a *subjective evaluation of something by someone* and it is fluently variable in time and by individual.

Your neighbor may be in an analogous circumstance, keeping chickens for eggs. They may be utterly uninterested in a fifth omelet of the day. By simple trading between you, the *real value* of those swapped foods has gone from zero to a seriously happy addition to each of your diets.

Create value. It benefits you *and* society. The free market provides the means for wealth creation, and each deal typically benefits both sides according to their lights. Value is *not* zero-sum.

4. The avoidance of selfishness is a higher-level issue, which comes about as a ramification of your moral creation of society (your choice to love those others you would, as yourself), your concern for this, your larger self. It is the fairness you would want for benefits and duties among those you care about. This is the noble and society-enhancing moral foundation, the *larger* self interest.

Chapter 12

Constructing and curating your greater self

So, I first focused on logically distinguishing you from your surroundings and accretions both conscious and passive, and all of this so you would know thyself. I distinguished/separated you (temporarily) from your attachments, so that you can acknowledge and also benefit from the distance and perspective this separation provides, and also demonstrated that fundamentally, below the vicissitudes and specificities of your chosen society and values, you at your core are real, axiomatic to your consciousness. I did aver, however, about the life/soul benefits which only those chosen attachments can provide. So now, I would like to return to the *choosing*, maintenance and evolution your attachments, of your greater self, that they be knowingly and optimally taken for the(your) greater good.

And I say *choosing* advisedly. I am thereby speaking as a partisan for conscious selfdom, self determination, encouraging the sovereignty of your individuality and freedom of choice, your sole and real authority.

For some attachments though, there may be no practical distinction between choosing and involuntary binding! I am encouraging your *attitude* of will, positivity, of personal freedom. In fact, from an external/objective perspective, such as a scientist trying to construct psychological experiments, there is no reliable way, when observing another's acts, to ever distinguish motivation between positive and negative, between will/desire and compulsion/need, even in the typical context of consciousness and agency assumed. Anyone can freely argue that you had to do something, or that you wanted to do that same thing, both for your own reasons, based on the meta-argument about whether you freely chose or were compelled to adopt those reasons. This therefore is not an argument of structural fact, it is an *attitudinal/political choice*. I am advocating that you take the positive internal psychological attitude of will and *considered, weighed desires*, rather than a perceived/chosen fatalism/compulsion, the exactly self-defeating notion that you are largely compelled and have no choice. I am on *your* side. It is this purely subjective positive attitude that will make a crucial difference in you. Even if the ultimate decision is the same.

And as I think while typing, the difference in how you decide a path, caused by this difference in attitude about your choosing, may be important/better one way or the other! Net philosophical neutrality, no easy answers! If a circumstance and decision is considered fatalistically/compelled, one may delay the decision because of its unattractiveness, and/or make it quickly. If the same decision was instead considered as voluntary and as self-profiting, one might spend more time weighing and comparing the options, grooming each to it's best light for the final choice. I am thinking there may be categories of choice that may be better done with one or other of those resulting side-effects... Wondering.

Sadly, there are some who illogically, but perhaps psychologically/situationally understandably do not love themselves, and who therefor would prefer the fatalistic/compulsion attitude, thereby diminishing their actual self and their volition from considerations, instead forging and living an externally-defined/judged identity. Erik Hoffer's book "The True Believers" describes how the most ardent joiners of parties and movements are those that hope to attain a social identity as the archetypal Communist, Democrat, gang member or such, exhibiting nothing personal, expending every effort to act and more importantly appear, in dress, rhetoric, and action as the model member, achieving this fungible social identity, escaping what may be an otherwise sad and uninspiring identity from the personal perspective. And again, there is sometimes a social environmental risk in taking an appreciable degree of self-determination at all. The more primitive and deprived the culture/economy, the more the ambient benefits will be tied to ones adherence to a group-assigned identity.

And I say *considered* because even with the most positive self-empowerment, one can love/choose unwisely: There are no easy answers. Our attachments are outside us, and only partially, if at all, under our control. And we do not know all about our attachments, and we do not know the future. We choose and hope for our attachments/loves, that they would be a buoy to our spirit (a buoy to our self). We form the the bind which lifts us. But this bond is in fact a neutral 'mechanical thing'. Depending on the shifting tides and directions of circumstance and your evolving directions, and the fate of those attachments, this bond may just as neutrally pull us down, where the buoy becomes an anchor. Thus it behooves us to soberly and periodically consider our bonds, their net benefits or deficits, and occasionally we may need/desire (and again, in all cases I prefer the attitude that it is your desire) to re-value them, investing more in some bonds, lessening others. And as we evolve in our morality and insight, this is both a self optimizing and self-evolving process. Your greater self is not fixed, it is an ongoing work of *art*.

And I say *art* because although you will/should use your best and evolving intellectual powers and your growing body of experience, these are the neutral tools and input to your aesthetic engine, what you evolvingly decide what is fair and beautiful. I think of the few major benefits of this book, particularly to those of modern Western culture, I hope to re-elevate the independent importance of aesthetics (for good and bad) in the consideration of human behavior and affairs. Morality is based on aesthetics.

Attachments are emphatically not simple inert possessions, nor are the bonds static. Your chosen attachments vary in their strength, in their benefits and in their risks. They are made with varying degrees of commitment, importance, duration, even individually varying cyclically in a day! For example, the practical Mother Theresa would periodically give preferential treatment to her narrow self, normally as all humans usually do, such as when she would eat all her own dinner, rather than instead always finding and feeding the always-extant more needy, if only by her rationalizing it (if she considered it) that she could do more good in the aggregate, for the poor, if she were alive and healthy, than if she were perpetually at the threshold of starvation in 'fairness'. Once she had her fill and was re-energized, we can see her rejoining the championing of her greater self, the poor. Also, the risks and benefits to us of our attachments are also not binary, but can and should be ranked by those two criteria, and each attachment weighed in that regard. This ranking is sometimes consciously chosen favoritism, for instance my own baldly averred preference for some forms of life over others. In my maximum greater self interest, I might still well consider trading off the extinction of an entire population, for instance of mosquitoes or polio viruses, in trade for a preferential and narrower benefit of my favorite species, man. There are also the less rationalized/considered choices made aesthetically, emotionally, subconsciously. We have all heard of teenage girls who have inadvertently killed themselves in car accidents by swerving off the road, rather than running over a beautiful and innocent squirrel darting onto the road. And we all make many of these emotional unconsidered allegiances second-to-second in a busy day, and we are governed/influenced in our behavior just as surely, just as subconsciously. B.F. Skinner has shown us how much more, and more reliably we are are as aesthetes and as subconsciously adherent to our current definition of self than we are what we are in actively consciously planning. His own subconsciously monitored desire for the attention of his lecture students was once comically manipulated by them when they conspired to visibly pay him more or less attention in class, according to how far left of the lectern he was. It is reported that Skinner found himself almost out the side door of the stage before he made the conscious self-observation and deciphered the trick! It remains a goal to be self-aware, to develop and foster the curiosity we hold about our self, to increase the degree by which we *can* modulate and modify our operant values. Don't leave it to a few times-in-a-lifetime where one takes stock and makes value adjustments. For some, their life will be much better served/lived if they dispassionately asked themselves why they felt (and reacted to) that 17th perceived minor annoyance of the day. Know thyself. A part of you will/can be constant, and chosen, for your whole life, and at the other end of the spectrum of you, another equally motivating and functional part of you changes, sometimes instant-to-instant.

Chapter 13

Shared identities: groups, states, cultures etc, and the contracts

We are a social animal. We survive and benefit by cooperative interaction. We see others as/like ourselves, and cooperate in assumed/understood 'contracts', expected reciprocal and hierarchical behaviors.

After/beyond the family, we extend ourselves to identify with group identities such as ' U.S. citizen', 'democrat', 'Muslim', 'employee of XYZ corp', etc. Importantly it should be noted that some of these groups may sometimes independently decide that you are or are not a member of their group, or some other group, whether you've chosen to belong, or not, or even know the group...

Groups have a main structure of a set of defined identities/roles for its members, defining internal and external properties and behaviors of each role/identity, but necessarily only being able to trade in/observe the external behavior of its members, hopefully inferring and encouraging the desired internal values.

These roles are structured stereotypes, with the intention of trustworthy functional behavior and interactions within the group 'machine'. Starting with a family, the 'father' has specific generic expectations placed on him, as does the 'mother', the 'child' etc. To the extent and seriousness with which the family(group) ethic/perspective is taken, these roles predominate, and any 'extraneous individuality' of the members is accepted only to the degree it does not conflict with the designated group-assigned responsibilities. Even the most 'progressive', 'liberal', 'world citizens' who speak of diversity as a strength, will hope/assume that any/all real diversity is orthogonal to the prime uniting group mission. And indeed and importantly this can be true in many cases, such as the desire that all skin colors are evident in their proportions, in sub-groups of value, such as as employees of government and business. But as soon as any diversity is exposed that is of direct relevance to the group ethos/identity, such as differing opinions on abortion among members of a church, or opinions on religion among members of a country's government, an omelet will be made, by cracking some eggs. Again, and simply, to the degree/strength that there is an agenda, either personal or group, diversity is polarized into the ignored/irrelevant, and the pro/

con (demanded/forbidden). Only when there is no agenda, no values, is everything is acceptable.

Enumerate and consider all the groups that you belong to, by passive inertial acceptance, personal choice, or unchosen, foisted on you by circumstance, or even personally rejected, but externally mandated and enforced. Each of these groups casts a different mold for you, some aspects maybe overlapping, but most unique to your role, and in some cases explicitly conflicting, either inadvertently or intendedly.

Tabulate the group-defined benefits you get from each group, the group-defined responsibilities/costs, and the tenor of your relationship: Did you enter into this contract as a full and free choice, or did you adopt it with less individual questioning, inertially initially accepting the benefits and then buying the responsibilities, or having it forced on you without any option or consideration allowed on your part.

These are the three criteria by which you should judge these contracts, and your attitude (diligence or minimum attention, projecting the values beyond the writ, or taking every loophole as an escape, etc) toward the expectations they place on you. It's going to be a personal weighing, and you may well have to make complex choices because of conflicts. And these choices may include 'voting with your feet' to leave the group (or at least its control), steering the group to a better course/identity, or even active subversion, such as in cases where exit is impossible and/or the group considers you a member, but its tenets have become anathema to you. You should not be a passive (at least not merely subconscious) accepter of each of these social contracts. You exhibit your identity and will, by being able to support your memberships and the relationships (the terms) in your own values. Even if it is to say "I am a such-and-such because I was born here and have no escape, and the only way to get what I personally value is to exhibit every indication of fervent adherence to my assigned role", that is rational. And this book may be more pain than good for some such, if only in that it encourages questioning in the cases where doubt alone diminishes the certainty of prospective rewards, and/or where any external evidence of questioning is a guarantee of social opprobrium of the worst kind.

And there is an angst to the spirit, to be expected when you are typecast for most of your day, or most of your life, by the requirements of a predominating contract/group, such as a job... Your ideal but impractical desire would be to be valued unconditionally for every dutiful or imaginative expression you create, if, when, and as you choose. This is most nearly approached in the closeness of a family, and especially for children, whose productive role is mostly unset. It is a common grief and rebellion of youth when they must transition from an essentially pampered centerplace of loving attention to a new junior position in the larger world where the benefits come from conformity to new social mores and groups, and particularly the jump to economic self-reliance, usually at the unprestigious bottom rungs of 'the machine'. Never were these youths as freshly steeped in love, and with as much self-worth, coupled by the cognitive dissonance, if not active rebellion against the rote-and-rule-based groups they must now join as beginners for their daily bread, some hoping that their shining individualities with their artful tattoos, deep grasp of the current music and party culture etc will (or *should rightly*) count for something, while the structures that are available to them are wanting first reliable loyalty to the economics, politics and functions of their entry-level roles.

And these human-created 'machines', corporations, governments, teams etc, are not evils. They are not new mistakes of Western culture. They are the only means to accomplish tasks that are more complicated and of wider scope than can be done by a loose network of self-interested individuals.

And yes, these human structures require hierarchy, both in specific merits and in executive roles. Leadership is agile to the degree it is concentrated, and the breakup of large complicated tasks into narrow subtasks with deep-and-specific experts is the logical productive design. There is no Eden, there never was past infancy, and no society can survive without the majority of its able members taking specific narrow roles/parts with sufficient commitment that the system as a whole can rely on them, producing enough real wealth/profit to pay their wage and significantly more, which goes to the overall production/output of the system. Even the deep aesthetes who assay to claim their worth is in their personal private feelings, are tethered practically to the market of otherwise disinterested individuals who freely appreciate the artists product, well enough to pay for it.

Chapter 14

On Meaning, Value, and Purpose

MEANING

Much has been done and said in the search for meaning. I think I can help, more so by precisely defining the terms and context than by supplying a prescriptive answer or direction. I define meaning as:

Meaning is the intended payload of a symbol.

An instance of meaning starts with a typically rich concept or image, often and crucially including an aesthetic value (good or bad). This often complex concept is then abbreviated/indexed/ tagged with a typically much simpler symbol, with the intent that the symbol can be more easily sent/received, even from and to ones self, as a shorthand and mnemonic, with the hope that the original full import of it is rehydrated/recalled in it's full feeling and function, actually perceived again, as needed.

As such, meaning is *not* intrinsic to things, not to the ink we use to represent a symbol. Meaning is a conscious (including subconscious) association made, and this is a personal act and entity. The item chosen as the symbol is inert, co-opted for the symbolizer's purpose. Meanings may be the same or different for the same symbol, for different individuals and different times. Life, the universe, the moon, a constellation, etc. are more elemental than symbols. They just *are*. They were not put there, just so, as symbols to convey a message to you, and it would be overweeningly egotistical to think so. If you choose to co-opt the sunset, or the moon, or the universe as a symbol, and attach a meaning to it, so that when ever after you contemplate or are exposed to your chosen symbol, the same meaning returns to you, that is the prerogative of your internal language, but it never infers/confers any change or objective state to/about the co-opted object itself. You may never be able to wear a particular sweater again because of the meaning it has for you, for instance if you know and despise someone who had owned it, but let some other person enjoy it, free of your emotional applique. They will not be 'infected'. It will not sadden them unless you saddle them with your meaning, and maybe not even then.

When someone asks what the meaning of life is, we should get clear on what the asker means by 'life'. If it is his own life so far, and as pondered in the future, the asker may be wondering about the sum total of his experiences, the goods and bads, and how to relate them to any overarching abiding agenda. I would guess that this person is in fact unclear/unsettled about their own agenda, and it would help them to review and build his/her collection of who/what he/she loves.

Now let's disambiguate and relate 'meaning' from 'value' or 'purpose'. The search for value is mistaken if it is done expecting/thinking that externalities have intrinsic values. I would define 'value' as:

Value is the perceived good/bad assigned to something, based on the agenda and aesthetics of the valuer, the perceived aid or block the object provides in the pursuit of the valuer's agenda and aesthetics.

Like 'meaning', value is also not intrinsic, it is consciously applied, and this association, this assigned quality exists only as/when/within consciousness and an agenda. Thus the 'value of life' is precisely and personally as much as you personally decide.

Now purpose. Purpose, like value also relates to agenda. Purpose is:

Purpose is the intended, newly imagined, or actualized utility of an object when/as/if manipulated or relied on in the furtherance of someone's agenda. It is, like value and meaning, subjective, determined/applied by the user, never inherent in the object itself. A given rock may have no purpose for one, be a weapon for another, and may serve as a keystone in the construction of another. Purpose is a quality applied, as manufactured by situational insight about the item to be purposed, in the light of an agenda being furthered..

But when people ask about the purpose of life, for instance, we should be careful to address the different definitions of life:

1. If 'life' is meant to mean 'The life of the asking individual', then the purpose of his/her life is to recognize/define/choose their identity, what they love, and to thereby define their agenda to express themself, furthering, expressing, and manifesting what they love.

2. If 'life' is meant to mean 'the whole networked biomass', then (and less differently than some would expect), it is the observed primary preoccupation (purpose, whether conscious or not) of life to self-express, where self is (most unifyingly) at the genetic level, reproducing an intended enduring identity beyond and across generations.

You will express yourself. This book is about the range and subtlety of how you would define that self.

Chapter 15

On Free Will...

First, and carefully, let's define the term, part by part.

Will - What is 'will', whether 'free' or not? Is it intent, desire, purpose? Or is it the power/ability to do something/anything? Is will distinct from the means and/or ability to enact an end?

When we use 'will' in the context of a last will and testament, the person clearly does not expect to have the ability to accomplish anything on the list of desires he/she has expressed in their will, and indeed the author of the list understands that it is be executed, if at all, when the author no longer exists. So, I would like us to consider will as one's abiding desires, one's agenda, whether the person can achieve them or not. For instance, someone's will could include that the Jews and Arabs shall tomorrow unite in friendship. There is an optimistic encouraging saying that "Where there is a will, there's a way". Putting aside the optimism for the moment, this reinforces and isolates the meaning of will, distinct from 'way or means', as resolute intent, non-whimsical enduring desires, whether there really is a way or not. So in short, let's use the synonyms 'intents' and 'desires' for 'will'.

Free - The general definition of 'free' is a good base: 'Separate from', 'not influenced by', 'costing nothing', 'unencumbered'. So now, when 'free' is applied to the term 'will/intent', what is it that our intents and desires are free of?

The most freedom we could define/approach would be that of absolute *randomness*, being free from all influence or pattern. And it should be obvious that is not the intent of the concept, as there is no benefit to 'will' with that level of freedom, 'random will', any more than the new Tesla would have a 'freedom' setting where it would automatically deliver random steering inputs. So what should our will, our purposes, our intents be free of? Certainly not our own intents, but what about compulsion and influence?

First let me deal with compulsion, which I will show to be a non-issue! Here is a dictionary definition of compulsion: com·pul·sion noun

1. the action or state of forcing or being forced to do something; constraint.

"the payment was made under compulsion"

2. an irresistible urge to behave in a certain way, especially against one's conscious wishes. "he felt a compulsion to babble on about what had happened"

We cannot absolutely control or predict what anything or anyone in the outside world can or will do to affect our circumstances, and our external circumstances are not our current subject of interest. The subject is our internal facility of 'free will'. And briefly, for completeness, if someone has a disability or malfunction such as Tourette's or worse, that imposes irresistible urges or acts on the person, though these are internal from a physical/medical/objective perspective, I will count them among external circumstances, external from a conscious/subjective will perspective.

One thing we can do, is to decide our *attitude* about the circumstances, and I propose that that makes a significant subjective/personal difference in the effort and type of our reactions to them, and the amount of will we manifest/perceive for ourselves:

I suggest that for every case where compulsion is claimed, we *could* instead choose the the opposite tenor/attitude of 'free self-interested choice'. Let's apply this theory to the example given in the definition:

"The payment was made under compulsion"

Let us suppose that a shopkeeper has made a payment to a local thug for 'protection services' to prevent any 'unfortunate accidents' from befalling his business. This is a clear picture of the thug threatening and coercing, sharply and materially changing and diminishing the shopkeeper's circumstances from what they were the day before, so that his choices are therefore also significantly different and worse than before he/she was targeted. As tragic and felonious as this happenstance is in its enactment, nevertheless, as soon as this shopkeeper understands his new reality (and let's assume for argument that there is no viable recourse/resistance he/she can engage to mitigate/reverse this 'life change'), he/she unchangingly *remains free* to compare and choose from his available options in this new and lesser normal. In a simple, typical weighing, according to his broad and unchanged self-interest (even if his/her circumstances have changed, his/her self-interests have not) he/she may logically craft his/her 'best win'; his/her best, now most profitable option. In this example, it is quite possible that the shopkeeper was calculatedly correct that making the protection payoff. But 'correct' is not the critical point here. What is critical is that he/she could believe and assert that his free will itself was unimpeded, and exercised personally in choosing his/her response.

We must distinguish and differentiate the pain and sorrow caused by diminishing/threatening changes in his circumstances from his unchanging ability to calculate and choose from whatever options he/she has. As such, except for his taking a defeated attitude or a continuingly self-confident attitude, his ability to choose, itself, remains unconstrained. As such, from a pure subjective/psychological perspective, I suggest you consider the option and ramifications of your *attitude*. You have the free choice of aesthetic, to 'feel compelled' or alternately to 'feel you have options to choose from', in any circumstance you face. In a case where you have no options, you have no choice to make, so free will is not relevant. And you are not free from loss. Circumstances may dictate such. But you remain free to choose among existing options.

Now let us address influence... Hearkening back to the silly random option, when you want to make a decision, you absolutely want to be influenced! You want your Tesla autopilot to be influenced by guard rails, cliffs and other vehicles, and an overall strategy of keeping you in one piece. In any decision-making process, you *want* to be informed and therefore influenced by all the relevant facts and risks regarding your options. As an example, fundamentally and typically, your personal agenda usually includes self-preservation as a continuing concern, so it very rightly figures in to, and influences some of your desires and goals and decisions. Exceptions to this, such as when someone decides to die for a cause are, I think, a significant example of free will, where the person has consciously chosen to weigh and be influenced by some social ideal and the value of his possibly changing the future of society by his act take precedence over the natural and normal concern for his own life.

But you would not like to be influenced by biased or faulty information, false promises etc... And that is very often a possibility, mandated by our non-omniscience and our limited and local circumstances and experiences, but these are also external factors, not an interesting factor in a free will discussion, except for the advised and continuing diligence one should have in obtaining and vetting relevant information, so as to be as correctly and fully informed, so as to be able to make as accurately intended choices as possible.

So, you want to be influenced, but when you are, we would suppose you'd at least want to be aware of it if you want to claim you possess the control implied by 'free will'. You might worry about *subconscious* influence, and there *is a lot* of that...

B. F. Skinner is the psychologist whose experiments amply showed how our established/pre-existing desires influence our behavior, continuingly, automatically, and subconsciously. A humorous and clear example is when the students in a psychology class, having Skinner himself as the teacher who had lectured them on the topic, decided to conspire. They agreed that during the next lecture, they would display animation, interest and participation in the lecture, in direct proportion to how far away from the lectern the professor was, banking safely on the professor's metabolized/ingrained/subconsciously monitored desire to be heard and attended in his class. On the chosen day, whenever he stood and talked at the lectern, it was all shoe-staring and 'crickets' but when he happened to step to the side, even in nervousness at the unusual blankness of his student's demeanors, the students would perk up as if the very word he'd just happened to say held the hidden key of his lecture. This teacher was unknowingly manipulated for a goodly period of the class, being influenced as far as his standing in the doorway of the lecture room while talking before he realized what was happening. :)

This anecdote is to clarify that you significantly program/record your general will in your mind and memory, your desires, your intents, your values into your memory and life-plan, in such a way that (and highly valuably so), they can control/influence your behavior subconsciously and semi-automatically, with or without your needing to be consciously aware of them. Indeed we all know of the overly-cerebral types, who have muted their impulses (through lack of attention and/or trust), their momentary unbidden unrationalized aesthetic reactions that serve others, the more 'intuitive types' to provide hints and deeper, or ulterior context to the current situation. These too-cerebrals will focus seriously, laser-like on the words spoken while a topic is being discussed, not reading the body language of the speakers, information which could and does inform others if a participant is being ulterior, deceitful or unserious, 'playing/trolling' the brainiac, who may never catch on.

It is absolutely important that you be self-aware of the constant subconscious judging you're doing, which delivers ready-mixed and full-color plausible stories and details about what is going on, and that there is great power in it. In a face-to-face situation, much of what you and the others communicate is non-verbal, even when you are not aware of it and are only conscious of your or their words. Even while you think and talk, pay attention to the emotional tone changes you go through, some surprising and unbidden. *You* may be saying something important and even counter-productive to your intent, with your body language and tone, unless you devote some self-awareness to the not-yet-rationalized emotional/aesthetic positions and reactions you are having while talking and listening, which are often clearly expressed to others by you, without your knowing.

And this revelation about your predominating and foundational subconscious influences is not to say that you are in fact unconscious most of the time, an automaton with all your awarenesses as after the-fact reports. For the most part, your rich and automatic intuition engine is very good about suggesting basic decisions, and you are indeed presented with them, to you in/as your live consciousness for your approval and action. You mostly act like the passive guard at a security desk, allowing most everything to pass after only a perfunctory gaze, as long as it looks reasonable, plausible on its face. And for those of your skills and action plans that you have long honed and well oiled with practice, those for which you may have developed and metabolized a very accurate and encompassing insight, your ability to accurately and fluidly, unresistingly pass, accept, and process your intuitions becomes notable for your seeming lack of intellectual involvement. Athletes and artists speak of 'being in the zone', 'unconscious', or 'out of body' where from a conscious self-aware perspective they observe they are performing flawlessly and fluidly, in the moment, not needing to make any conscious rationalized decisions. This semi-puzzled in-awe sense of self-alienation is because they are not aware enough of (or do not sufficiently credit) their own always-on sub-linguistic interpretation/

intuition engine, which when honed and practiced, delivers rich and practically real time decisions and action plans that we need only follow.

However, as a philosopher and free mind, you should also absolutely monitor and double-check your 'intuition engine', especially when the stakes are high. It is in these occasional and effortful self-called timeouts, where you perhaps follow a moment of doubtful/careful hunch, or perhaps you have decided to hold a specific discipline of self-checking in the given context, or perhaps you become aware of a cognitive dissonance between the current plausible plot as it has been presented to you, and some current, as yet inchoate troublement you feel. Follow that feeling and find the source of incoherence. There will be such times when you come to decide that the values that governed your typical auto-pilot evaluations are skewed or obsolete, based on your new evaluation. It is at these rare times where you make conscious, serious permanent adjustments to your base values or understandings that you manifest the freest will. After your change, thenceforth your newly-reprogrammed intuition engine will take up your new course/values. It is in these occasional adjustments we make that our 'free will' is most evident, after which you can newly confidently return to your newly improved preprogrammed subconscious reactions.

To put a fine point on this, these values of yours, which you occasionally add to, alter, or hone, are your identifications. These are the makings of your self, and as previously described, they run a gamut/spectrum from trivial or instant-to-instant judgments that you can freely change in a trice, to biologically-based ones that most people never reweigh, to those that some who decide they will die for a cause, do. I submit that your 'free will' is identical to your freedom/willingness to change *you*, your identifications, what you love, in what proportions. Once and while your values are fixed, an autopilot mode which you more passively watch/follow, predominates.

So, this subconscious always-on influence engine part of your mind is there, like it is in all sentient animals, to provide instant pre/subconscious judgments which present themselves to you in rich and redolent real-time plausibility, the goosebumps felt, and animal attractions or animal repugnances felt, and only afterwards do we engage if at all, in any rationalization of the judgment. More often we react instantly and unquestioningly, even subconsciously as above, and our only rationalization is a simple recounting of the likely story that was interpreted. What we have pared down as 'free will' is a rare and effortful act in our day-to-day lives.

For a singularly brilliant and seminal book on this topic, I recommend 'Thinking, Fast and Slow' by the Nobel prize-winning Kahneman. It is the one book for which I pulled out all my 'father cards' to impose/wheedle that my children must read it.

The viable concern with influence is then mostly only when we are influenced by values we hold but are not aware of, or do not know consciously to be currently involved. This is never to be fully avoided, but free will is a *goal*, a direction, not a yes-or-no binary condition. Know thyself, study yourself carefully and often, so that your self-direction be as well (and consciously) informed/influenced as possible.

So, your capability of free will is the areas in which, and the degrees with which you can change your values, what/who you identify with, functionally who you are, your operant identity/self. It's all Skinner from there on down. And the degree of your actual expressed free will is the degree to which you:

1. know your relevant operant values/identity, the changeable ones and the unchangeable ones. So in one arena of action/decisions you may well know all the relevancies about yourself, and may be totally free to know and express why you're making a given decision, while in another arena you may know less about yourself, such perhaps as how your never-known experiences/treatment as a toddler affects your gut reaction to dogs or women with red hair. and

2. actually re-examine your values when you experience and/or feel something that puts them in conflict, initially only as the inchoate discomfort, the 'cognitive dissonance' when you're aware that something's not right, then you rationalize the conflict and resolve it with a shift/editing of you, your values. Detect and cure your incoherencies.

And 'free will' is like a muscle. Within limits, it is developable and can be made stronger with discipline and practice. It is a personal conscious hygiene and attitude of continuing self-determination.

It is not something that can be defined/tested 'objectively', from without. There are two opposite presumptions, that the test subject is conscious (presuming/assuming what that means 'objectively') or that the subject is not really conscious, that his/her reactions are deterministic and that their 'experience' is a side-effect after the fact/reaction. Each of these is eternally moot, and any external psychological test will have to assume one as one of the initial bases, fatally biasing and pre-ordaining the test results: Either the subject is in final charge, or not.

THE TECHNICAL REQUIREMENTS FOR FREE WILL

In order to have free will, one must be able to consider and attend factors beyond the raw input of the 'now'. One must be able to anticipate, to be able to form, evaluate and react to a model of the future. Indeed to posit and compare alternative projected futures, so as to inform a choice. Even in such a small case as catching (or ducking) a fly ball, one must predict and time the trajectory, so as to occupy (or vacate) an intercepting location ahead of time. We do not, cannot continuingly follow the flying ball as it approaches. We must take an instant to predict far enough ahead that our slower body can then move to the predicted intercept point before the faster ball reaches it. Without the free 'scratch' memory devotable to positing relevant futures, we will only be able to directly and simply react to inputs. And of course the memory (in the computer sense) is just the canvas. The ability to draw a specific image or images of the future is needed. These (and all) futures are all objectively non existent, illusions. That is all they have to be, in order to serve their purpose. Then the author can choose among them, and craft his response appropriately.

THE DOWNSIDES OF FREE WILL

Free will is the conscious, personal stand/attitude, that one will remain free to judge and choose. I generally advocate (preach?) self-determination, a positive self-confident attitude, but I must also establish the inexorable 'philosophical neutrality' of it, as for all 'attitudes', the cons to the pros, the cases where it is inappropriate.

1. Free will also imparts responsibility, and there are people and circumstances where this is a burden and risk. As in the case I described above where a performer like an athlete, jazz musician or race car driver find their best abilities by their giving rein to their pre-honed and tuned instincts and motor memory, not often imposing or even considering higher-level executive decisions, because such considered oversight takes precious time, second-for-second where ones attention is necessarily removed from the informative sights and sounds of ones raw inputs, to look inward, if only for an instant, to consider a model (or even language!) to manipulate for decision-making, and such diversions from the real-time inputs can miss miss or mis-time important inputs and therefore important reactions. And in the longer-term scope, there are people who wish to avoid individual solitary considerations, and who may even have a history where on the occasions they stood and chose to make sole executive decision, the outcome

was poor, so they have come to mistrust themselves. There are some cultures/economies where the amount of cooperation required is constant and high, and under those conditions, social identity and bonds are more paramount, so things are looked at more in terms of obligations rather than individual choices. And in poor circumstances where there is little viable choice, free will is de-emphasized.

2. Wielding free will takes time and attention away, if only temporarily, from what is happening externally, and this delay may be ungraceful, harmful or even fatal when an immediate and sensitive undoubting reaction to the revealing circumstances would have saved the cerebral's life.

A DISPUTE:

When someone pondering desserts says

"I've decided I'll have the vanilla, not the strawberry."

Someone can easily claim compulsion:

"You didn't really choose, you *had* to do that." and the chooser would say

"No I didn't have to! I could have chosen strawberry, I just slightly prefer vanilla".

But the accuser will say

"Ah, but did you *choose* to like vanilla more? Aren't you compelled by your tastes?".

And the chooser can say

"No, I am free at any time to change my tastes for any reason. I could have decided not to choose vanilla, because I didn't like what it implied to others about my lack of adventurousness or sophistication." and the retort

"So you were then simply compelled by other external forces and your then-competing values to change your attitude toward vanilla!" and:

"No, I just chose to reconsider and reweigh those competing values at this time, even though they may have been there always."

I believe this sort of back-and-forth example could be extended indefinitely with matched players.

This necessary presumption from without, about a subject's volition or compulsion (either direction; another sympathetic observer could have agreed with the dessert chooser about his volition) will doom psychological experiments that purport to detect unconscious/involuntary 'choice' before the subject is aware of making a decision. No matter how deeply into the brain that scientists may detect and correlate brain activity with a given choice, posited to occur before the subject is aware of making a choice, we can answer simply that this detected pre-conscious activity is the workings of the pre/subconscious 'intuition engine', and that this resulting output is then delivered later to the consciousness of the subject as input, where he/she typically then acknowledges/accepts/avers it. As such, the subject *could* also have then taken a moment to decide against it. These bio tests then become as unrelevatory as if they monitored your nerves in your legs, and declared that they could detect and predict when you'd say 'ouch', in between the time they surreptitiously hit your toe with a hammer, and when the nerve impulses passed their detection zone and went on to reach your brain.

And if these tests are to be fair, because they are purporting to test conscious decisions, the subject, the decider should be fully informed. They should be told that if they say ouch, or say they like the picture of the puppy, it will be taken as evidence of their lack of real decision-making power. I suspect that then a few self-standing subjects might just lie, if only to provide support-ive (if subversive) evidence of free will. And most of these tests provide trivially simple cases such as 'does this hurt?' or 'how do you feel pictures of puppies or severe injuries?', where the sub-conscious status quo is plenty sufficient for the right answer. A better but more complicated problem set would present plausible *but wrong* first impressions, with right answers that are only arrived at by an overriding executive decision to doubt and test. Any correct answers to such necessarily-considered questions would favorably hint at 'free will'.

I will try to get the permanent link to a study which divided a large group of test subjects by two criteria: 1 - basic intelligence as currently defined/measured by IQ tests, and 2 - by whether the subject was religious or not. Then for each band of similarly intelligent people, a range of appropriately easy/hard but acces-sible problems were given them. The test results showed one and only one particular class of problem that differentiated religious people from non-religious ones, across the board. Only in the cases of a problem, which had a reachable answer, but which had a first-blush plausible but wrong answer, it was the religious people who more often went with their first gut plausibility-engine-generated reaction/answer.

I wish the study went into timing too, because I would predict that the religious (if we continue to bear the test implication) would have finished their tests faster. This is not only because they skipped the time-consuming analysis required to disprove the first guess, but that they also didn't waste time calculating and questioning when the right answer was readily apparent. The doubters may well have wasted time double-checking the obvious. So neither bias is purely better or worse. They are philosophically neutral, and only omniscience about the relevant circumstances of any decision would allow the decider to correctly choose which attitude to adopt.

Another point of the dispute example is that there is an emotional, psychological, subjective (and very important) aesthetic difference between the two possible 'tones' while you are decision-making. This is certainly influenced by the aesthetic aspect of the choices, and the aesthetic judgment of the overall circumstances, not necessarily even relevant to the choice itself. If the general circumstances are deemed good by a healthy happy individual choosing between taking the lottery winnings in a lump sum or in yearly payments, the chooser may feel energized and optimistic and attracted to figuring out the best path. On the other hand, a person, severely pressured for other reasons might feel put upon having to make the same decision, and maybe take a shortcut gut-guess to decide, rather than devote energy. And of course choosing between two negative options is often made in a bad mood, and done in overall onerous situations, and one feels pressed and innervated, wishing it would all go away. But this is meta. The actual process and calculation of relative merit of any set of choices is similar. Options are weighed according to the choosers values at the time, and the best/least-bad option chosen.

I suggest that determining the tone/sense of compulsion/promise that you take on during a decision is separate choice you can make about yourself, and I suggest that the tone affects the type and process of the resulting decision.

"The more important a decision is, the more critical it is to treat it as a game" - unknown

Chapter 16

Correspondences with a fearless thinker

This is a series of correspondence between Josh Rasmussen and me. I will put his responses in Italics. He is a brilliant and fearless philosopher, and author of "How Reason Can Lead to God". I show this conversation as a fruitful application of the ideas, exactitudes, and strictures objective/subjective dualism, producing more clarity and dissolving logical over-reaches.

From Josh:

Hi Joe,

In our other exchange, we have been examining your system. I'd like to share with you an element of my system, since it is related to yours. It's about the universality of reason.

I begin with a definition: "x is similar in some respect to y" means "x has something in common with y." (If someone says that x is similar to y yet has nothing in common with y, then I have no idea what they are saying, or what they've said is a contradiction.)

Next I observe that some logical thoughts are similar to others. For example, my thought this morning that A=A, for any A is similar to my thought right now that A=A, for any A.

We then deduce, by definition of "similarity," that some logical thoughts have something in common. For example, the thoughts I mentioned above have something in common. Since both thoughts are about identity, let us call what they have in common "The Law of Identity."

The next thing to see is that The Law of Identity is distinct from my individual thoughts about identity. That's because my individual thoughts are distinct from each other. To see this inference clearly, consider my thought this morning about identity. That thought is is not the same thought as my more recent thought about identity. The thoughts are similar (maybe even exactly similar), but they are not one and the same thought. Yet, if these individual thoughts were the The Law of Identity, then they would be one and the same thought. But they aren't the same thought. So they are not The Law of Identity. Q.E.D.

So far we have established from my starting definitions that the Law of Identity is distinct from my individual thoughts about identity. In other words, the Law of Identity transcends my individual thoughts about identity.

You might wonder how I can access the Law of Identity if it transcends my particular thoughts. The answer is that I access the Law of Identity via my inner awareness of the law. It's like if I'm touching a larger pillar with my hands. My hands touch the pillar, while the pillar exists even when my hands are not accessing it.

While it is possible that there is no pillar beyond my experience, it is not possible that there is no Law of Identity beyond my awareness of it, for I just proved that the Law of Identity exists distinct from my individual thoughts about identity.

So far this result is established by crystal clear deduction from definition. I will now give a larger picture of the result for the sake of illustration. This picture is not part of the deduction. It is just a way of seeing one way of understanding it.

Imagine an abstract landscape that consists of logical lines. The logical lines include basic laws of thought, including The Law of Identity and The Law of Non-Contradiction. It also includes inferences from those laws. Different minds access this landscape from within their own minds. When you access the abstract landscape, you have a thought in your own mind. The thought is like a scope that sees the abstract landscape.

Some people mistake their own scope for the reality they see. They think, for example, that The Law of Identity they see just is their latest thought about identity. But I've already shown that the Law of Identity is not the same as the individual thoughts about identity. The thoughts are scopes that see the abstract landscape.

People from different cultures, times, and homes can explore the abstract landscape using their own minds. Different people see different parts of the landscape, but different people can also see some of the same parts. This explains progress in mathematics. As different minds record some of the same discoveries, they can help other minds find their way to the same crevices in the logical landscape.

In summary, there are principles of logic that differ from individual thoughts of them. This result follows from the meaning of "similarity" together with the observation that individual logical thoughts are similar to each other. We may call the totality of the principles of reason "the logical landscape."

It's been fun exploring the logical landscape with you. :)

Best wishes,

Josh

Joe:

This is good work we're doing.

"I begin with a definition: "x is similar in some respect to y" means "x has something in common with y." (If someone says that x is similar to y yet has nothing in common with y, then I have no idea what they are saying, or what they've said is a contradiction.)"

Clear so far.

"Next I observe that some logical thoughts are similar to others. For example, my thought this morning that A=A, for any A is similar to my thought right now that A=A, for any A. "

OK... Is the similarity of the two thoughts anything different than that their expressions are identical? Need it be? If Mabel's thought on Sunday that "Gladys thinks she's all that, but everyone knows she looks ridiculous with her big hair" is identical to her thought on Monday when she said as much to Eunice and the rest of the girls, this thought is unchanging... ;)

"We then deduce, by definition of "similarity," that some logical thoughts have something in common. For example, the thoughts I mentioned above have something in common. Since both thoughts are about identity, let us call what they have in common "The Law of Identity." "

OK, and the thoughts I added can be included in the body of work called "The Laws Of Gladys Trying To Make Herself Out To Be Special, And That It's All A Big Joke". ;)

"The next thing to see is that The Law of Identity is distinct from my individual thoughts about identity. That's because my individual

thoughts are distinct from each other. To see this inference clearly, consider my thought this morning about identity. That thought is is not the same thought as my more recent thought about identity. The thoughts are similar (maybe even exactly similar), but they are not one and the same thought. Yet, if these individual thoughts were the The Law of Identity, then they would be one and the same thought. But they aren't the same thought. So they are not The Law of Identity. Q.E.D."

I am not sure what is being asserted then proven, but yes, the two thoughts are identical in function, but distinct temporally, even if only in the one necessary mind, yours. Yes, the thought "A=A" is not the thought 'The Law Of Identity'. "The Law Of Identity" is a separate thought, a concept, a label, a qualification, a generalization you can assign to, or assert about any instance of "A=A", or "B=B" etc. You are considering (necessarily) *your* Law Of Identity.

"So far we have established from my starting definitions that the Law of Identity is distinct from my individual thoughts about identity. In other words, the Law of Identity transcends my individual thoughts about identity."

No. It does not transcend. It simply exists separately and independently. A person can know and employ the self-assurance/ discipline that "A=A', even implicitly by holding such analogously true for every symbol he/she uses in an algebraic proof, one that might not use the symbol 'A' at all, without explicitly stating/holding that "A=A", though he/she would have to if they were in an axiomatic math class. Absent that irritating class, there is no need for, no transcendence of, the generality or the label when using/thinking/assuming "A=A", and symmetrically there is no transcendence or need for "A=A" when pondering The Law Of Identity. This, your Law is simply a different generality, about defining sets, about identity/similarity, about a different subject than is the law that A=A. I would define the LOI as 'all propositions that are/can be expressed identically, whether distinguished by having been expressed by the same person at different times, or identically by others, shall be deemed to act/function/mean the same in their respective contexts. This can be seen as a detailed, specific case of 'A=A', where in this case 'A' stands for a given thought. As such, it would seem that the more general 'A=A' transcended the more specific LOI, if we take 'transcend' to mean 'be more general, more widely applicable' etc. In no conceivable way has any of this hinted at proving anything outside, anything abiding beyond/except as/when you entertain/remember it.

"You might wonder how I can access the Law of Identity if it transcends my particular thoughts. The answer is that I access the Law of Identity via my inner awareness of the law. It's like if I'm touching a larger pillar with my hands. My hands touch the pillar, while the pillar exists even when my hands are not accessing it. "

No, it does not transcend your particular thoughts. It *is* one of your particular thoughts at the time(s) you consider it, and it is harmlessly non-existent otherwise, as are all your other thoughts. I would put it better, more simply, that you access *any* law whenever you want, by your creation/re-creation/remembering it. Yes, you are aware of it, from whenever you formulated it, and whenever you remember it. No 'pillar', no idea exists as such, except as/when you actively posit it in live thought. You do rely on your memory to symbolize it, from which you can reconstitute it easily when needed, no different than the notes you might prepare for an examination that allowed such. It is you who deems which ideas are fundamental and which are filigrees, according to your own classifications, also ideas. And these may be changed over time. Some people change their lives radically by their promoting or demoting or replacing their chosen 'pillars'.

"While it is possible that there is no pillar beyond my experience, it is not possible that there is no Law of Identity beyond my awareness of it, for I just proved that the Law of Identity exists distinct from my individual thoughts about identity."

As above, the Law of Identity and the Laws Of Gladys need only exist as/when you hold them and remember them. No transcendence of your mind needed or possible, let alone evident. No proof at all that any law/proposition exists independent of your awareness of, positing it.

Josh replies, quoting me:

"This is good work we're doing."

Yes! :) And it is special for truth-seekers to come together like this. This is what good philosophy is all about. :)

"OK... Is the similarity of the two thoughts anything different than that their expressions are identical? Need it be? If Mabel's thought on Sunday that "Gladys thinks she's all that, but everyone knows she looks ridiculous with her big hair" is identical to her thought on Monday when she said as much to Eunice and the rest of the girls, this thought is unchanging... ;)""

Sure, as long as "identical" meets the definition above about something being in common. Philosophers call this "type" identity, as opposed to "token" identity.

"I am not sure what is being asserted then proven, but yes, the two thoughts are identical in function, but distinct temporally."

Translation: type identical but not token identical.

For whatever it may be worth, I would think your system will end up denying my starting definition -- or working with a different definition.

Joe:

"Sure, as long as "identical" meets the definition above about something being in common. Philosophers call this "type" identity, as opposed to "token" identity."

I would put it more simply/clearer, that "A=A" in the morning, and "A=A" in the afternoon, and "B=B" are instances/specific examples of a generality, in which the author of the general defines/decides the relevant commonality. The generality you cite in this case is the 'law of identity'. If instead you defined 'the law of syntactically coherent equations', "A=B" would also qualify as an example. 'Type identity' should be equated to 'member of the set/class' of semantically identical thoughts', such as any/all expressions of 'A or not-A'

"Translation: type identical but not token identical. "

I can grasp 'type identical' as 'like members, functionally identical in their respective places, according to the criteria of the set/generality', and I guess by 'not token identical', you mean 'not one thing', which we agree on. But that term 'token identical' seems inept because 'token' implies 'symbol', such that the symbol 'A' may stand for something different in one context than another, even though the token is the same. We don't want that extra distraction. To be clear for our purposes, I would instead use a better term that clearly implies 'the functionally/semantically same exact thing, independent of the label, in its context'. If that is precisely what philosophers mean by 'token identical' then I will hold my nose against the butchery of English, and make the conversion in my mind... (;) * 0.5 because I find much targeted deception and self-deception find their camouflage in co-opted 'special' meanings of common English words)

"By "transcend," I just meant "distinct" -- as in not token identical."

OK, but then "A=A" in the morning also 'transcends' "A=A" in the afternoon, and that removes the difference that might have been valuable between a specific instance (A=A) and the generality that which we might label as "The Law Of Identity". So I'd avoid the term 'transcend' because one might imply/hope for some sort of intrinsic temporal difference in duration between some ideas as you'd mentioned. That does not exist. I assert again, that ideas exist only as/when you entertain them, for only as long as you entertain them. You may tokenize/symbolize them to aid in your remembering them, and this may be on paper or in your memory, but they only (re) exist as the actual functional ideas after you re-assert them after refreshing yourself from memory.

It does not transcend your particular thoughts. And except for the posited-by-faith existence of 'other', something independent of your mind, *nothing* transcends(in the more common meaning of the word) your particular thoughts. Without that first leap of faith, *everything* is your particular thoughts.

"Just to clarify, my proof establishes non token identity (not one and the same as). At least, that how it looks to me. My higher goal is to clarify things, if I can. :)"

Good enough, but so far it's simple in our ability to define generalities, sets whose membership requires that the elements/members be identical according to whatever our chosen criteria. For a silly example, one could say that A=A is not 'type-identical' with 'a=a' because the set criteria include the font and capitalization as well as semantics.

"For whatever it may be worth, I would think your system will end up denying my starting definition -- or working with a different definition. "

I don't think so, not in this case anyway. At least if you can see the sameness of my alternative nomenclature 'general' and 'specific/instance', the set analogy, which I think that establishes the in-*common* identity.

Josh:

Okay. A few quick notes:

1. I agree that philosophers sometimes use terms poorly. We have a problem with that. :)

2. The rhetorical device "posited by faith" expresses your perspective. That is, you see no evidence / support for the result I propose. But of course, that doesn't capture my own perspective. I think the result follows from my definitions. If I have made a mistake, it is an honest mistake. It's like if I say the wall is green because it looks green to me. The wall might not look green to you, but that doesn't mean I am positing by faith that the wall is green. Maybe I'm just looking at the wrong wall or a different one, or maybe I have something green in my eye. :)

3. I am not quite sure what else to say. We agree that types differ from individuals ("tokens"). We also agree that different individual thoughts could belong to the same type T. So, by the law of transitivity, T is not one and the same as those individual thoughts. I think we might even agree there.

A further point is that for each individual thought, T can exist without that particular thought. Proof: individual members of T exist without each other (e.g., your morning thoughts about the Law of Identity exist without your afternoon thoughts about the Law of Identity, yet those individual thoughts do not exist without T (e.g., T exists when you have your morning thoughts of identity and when you have your afternoon thoughts of that same type); therefore, for each individual thought, T can exist without that thought (e.g., T exists without your morning thought of identity).

Best,

Josh

Joe:

Thanks!

"1. I agree that philosophers sometimes use terms poorly. We have a problem with that. :)"

Yes, it is an aspect of our pursuit that some of the scaffolding terminology as we climb becomes obsolete/imprecise, and we must amend/clarify/replace them. I am saddened to see some whole 'schools' of philosophy where folks collect to participate in a supportive 'karaoke of term-of-art juggling', with archaic concepts that survive only where they are not rigorously clearly defined and logically challenged. And some people stay there primarily because their favored hoped-for world-views remain supported by the degrees of imprecision and hidden incoherence that the archaic terms allow.

"2. The rhetorical device "posited by faith" expresses your perspective. That is, you see no evidence / support for the result I propose. But of course, that doesn't capture my own perspective. I think the result follows from my definitions. If I have made a mistake, it is an honest mistake. It's like if I say the wall is green because it looks green to me. The wall might not look green to you, but that doesn't mean I am positing by faith that the wall is green. Maybe I'm just looking at the wrong wall or a different one, or maybe I have something green in my eye. :)"

I am not using the phrase 'posited by faith' as a rhetorical device. I intend it to be exact. Unless we can logically defeat the reasonable doubt illustrated by the core point of solipsism, that *all* may be just your imagination, it remains a leap of faith to presume *anything* distinct from, let alone transcendent of you and your thoughts/images. If you say 'the wall is green', we can agree that this is an example of posited 'raw sensory input', and leave the perceived greenness per se, as experientially axiomatic. If you or I say something was warm, green, and beautiful, none of those attributes are questionable, none posited by faith. What is subject to faith/doubt is the structural interpretation of the experience, such as whether there really is a wall there, as opposed to an optical illusion, or a rectangular patch on a screen, etc. The song is beautiful, but she singing? Lip-syncing? Is there someone really there, or just a projection? Is that bright light the end of the tunnel, or a train headlight coming this way? Is that water or a mirage? And yes, if either of us makes mistakes, we shall know them to be honest, for sure, and we shall be grateful for clarifications.

"3. I am not quite sure what else to say. We agree that types differ from individuals ("tokens"). We also agree that different individual thoughts could belong to the same type T. So, by the law of transitivity, T is not one and the same as those individual thoughts. I think we might even agree there."

Sure. 'Types' are sets, generalizations, and 'tokens' are examples/members. And yes, the concept of the set that includes all thoughts, is itself a thought... But again, the general definition/categorization that defines a given set 'T' is merely a separate idea from any of the ideas it contains, and any mind can simply and separately wield an idea that is a member of the set, or the idea of the set, dependent on the relevance to his/her current drift. Someone may profitably exploit a specific example of "A=A" repeatedly for an entire lifetime without ever generalizing to "A=A" (for all 'A's) or needing to. Similarly, we could define a set T of all instances of a proposition X, and as per 'LOI', every 'X' shall be semantically/functionally identical in its context, but we need not ever define the specific/unique semantics of 'X'. Set and member are distinct, but neither precedes the other, nor depends on the other.

"A further point is that for each individual thought, T can exist without that particular thought. Proof: individual members of T exist without each other (e.g., your morning thoughts about the Law of Identity exist without your afternoon thoughts about the Law of Identity, yet those individual thoughts do not exist without T (e.g., T exists when you have your morning thoughts of identity and when you have your afternoon thoughts of that same type); therefore, for each individual thought, T can exist without that thought (e.g., T exists without your morning thought of identity)."

Again, as above, T and any other thought, even if the other thought is a member of that T can separately exist.

Josh:

"So, does any disagreement remain?"

There is this: on my definitions, not only can the Law of Identity (the type) exist without your individual logical thoughts about identity, it can exist even without you. That is because we have thoughts that are of the same type. This follows from my definition of "similarity" (in terms of sharing something in common), together with your own premise that we at least have similar thoughts. Do you take these steps?"

Joe:

"No. The LOI can exist as a logical thought in my mind, without my positing any specific members, such as my thoughts about identity. That LOI cannot exist without me, though. If I posit another mind, like yours, and that I posit that you are considering 'the' LOI, then I would believe that both of our LOI conceptions were identical. As you say, *similar*, (mind-invariant, ideally), but not a singular object. And purely, exactly subjectively, *nothing* exists without me, and there is logically no way I could prove it, even if there is plenty of statistical evidence to disallow any doubt on my part, from a practical/heuristic basis.

Again, your grasp (instance of) LOI is distinct, though functionally identical to mine, and to yours at another time, but each of these is temporally separate, and in the case of 'us', separately private to each of us. The LOI is just another example of an idea that can be collected by you into a set T, when/as you need.

Josh:

Just to be sure, when I say they are "similar," it follows from my definition of "similar" (in terms of sharing something in common), that there is something in common between those thoughts. That is true whether the thoughts are individual thoughts in your mind or *whether they are scattered across many minds. If any thoughts are similar, then they have something in common. This something in common is not the same as any individual members, whether those members exist in your mind or mine.*

Now one could deny that my thoughts are even similar to yours. But then that means my thoughts have nothing in common with yours, in which case we cannot communicate.

There is much to celebrate, including progress in this exchange.

So here's a hypothesis about your thought process. You are seeing first that logic has the nature of a thought. And you are also seeing this thought-like nature from within your own mind. These sights within your mind lead you to infer that logic is one of your thoughts. But now that the spotlight is on this inference, you can ask yourself if it is correct. That is, does it follow from the fact that (i) logic has the nature of a thought, and (ii) you see logic from within your mind, that therefore logic is one of your thoughts?

My argument has been that logic (true logic) cannot be reduced to your own individual thoughts because it can exist without them. It can exist without them because someone besides you can follow true logic (for example, I can reason correctly), even while you are eating pizza and having no thoughts about logic at all. Now you will say that my true logic is different from yours. My response is that at least they are similar, and that they cannot be similar unless they have something in common. This something in common is an example of something that can exist without its individual members. This example verifies the problem with the inference above.

I predict: more progress is ahead. :)

Joe:

Similarity is a quality defined in the mind of the comparer, the definition of a set. Correct, the class/set defined by the criteria the comparer chooses for similarity is a different object than the items compared (thoughts in this case). Nothing in any of this hints at anything beyond the contents/products of those minds.

"So here's a hypothesis about your thought process. You are seeing first that logic has the nature of a thought."

No. Logic, as exemplified, not as thought about, is a 'mechanical integrity', coherency between thoughts.

"And you are also seeing this thought-like nature from within your own mind."

I *only* see things in my mind.

"My argument has been that logic (true logic) cannot be reduced to your own individual thoughts because it can exist without them."

I am never reducing logic (the quality of coherency, non-contradiction of related thoughts) to my own individual thoughts. I try to attain logical consistency *between* my related thoughts. But logic, (the quality of coherency, non-contradiction of related thoughts) cannot and need not exist without some set of related thoughts. Logic per se is not the same as the concept of logic.

"It can exist without them because someone besides you can follow true logic (for example, I can reason correctly), even while you are eating pizza and having no thoughts about logic at all."

Well, sure, but logic is still not exemplified without some mind or other positing a set of related ideas that interact/relate, and produce no contradictions. In the example you give, it is *your* thoughts that cohere, such as while your observing me mindlessly cramming pizza, and logically concluding I was raised by wolves... Logic is mind-invariant, not mind-independent. Boxing can exist without your fists, because someone else can be punching people with their fists. No transcendence of 'fistdom' though...

"Now you will say that my true logic is different from yours."

Your logic and mine (and our very occasional illogic) are certainly of our own production.

"My response is that at least they are similar, and that they cannot be similar unless they have something in common."

Yes, and as above, this commonality is defined solely according to the chosen criteria of the comparer. This is nothing more or transcendent of any other mental categorization effort. Two protons are not 'similar' or 'different' except as compared and deemed so according to the chosen criteria. For instance if I were to present the significantly non-zero statistical likelihood of a given oxygen molecule anywhere on earth now, was one that had once been breathed by Hitler, and was going to be in someone's next breath, there are *many* who would deem that molecule as significantly different than others, and would hold their breath and go elsewhere to breath that next breath.

"This something in common is an example of something that can exist without its individual members."

Sure. As above, we have no argument that the categorization/identification criteria for an item can exist without there even ever being any satisfying element. But that does not hint at, let alone prove that the definition of 'in common', this chosen similarity is anything more/beyond a personal conscious construct of the individual comparing mind. That would sound like the archaic proto-philosophical concepts like 'essence', where the object was mistakenly considered to hold/emanate some key, narrowed identity. In reality, objects just are, in total. 'Essence' is an intellectual simplification of the object, deciding which attributes are important to the viewer for their purpose/aesthetics, and which attributes are to be ignored/discounted.

"This example verifies the problem with the inference above."

Did I successfully disown any problematic inference?

Josh:

Thanks, those are good clarifications.

"mind-invariant, not mind-independent "

A point of agreement.

The place for further progress, I think, is in the implications of mind-invariance. I'm content to leave it here for now.

Roads for progress:

1. Teasing out the implications of mind-invariance.

2. Distinction between mind-dependence vs. local-mind-dependence (i.e., dependence on the mind that apprehends or instantiates logic).

3. More on types vs. particulars in relation to (2).

Okay, I can't resist. Why not have this fun on my b-day. :)

Taking road (3), on types vs. particulars. Suppose two computers A and B share software S. S can exist without A, since if A were destroyed, S would still exist in B. Same in the other direction: if B were destroyed, then S would exist in A. So S doesn't depend locally on A, and S doesn't depend locally on B. What is true for software is also true for logical consistency. Both A and B are logically consistent. So they share logical consistency in common. Again, logical consistency -- the type -- is not the same as any token/particular logical consistency.

I hope these thoughts serve your system, or at least thoughts "similar" to mine. :)

Best wishes,

Joe:

"Roads for progress:"

Ready and eager!

"1. Teasing out the implications of mind-invariance." A fundamental crucial distinction between it and 'mind-independence'. The primary implication of mind-invariance is the similarity of the minds.

2. Distinction between mind-dependence vs. local-mind-dependence (i.e., dependence on the mind that apprehends or instantiates logic)." Yes, there is always a possibility of parallax, artifacts based on the singularity/locality of private perspective. To the extent we differ in experiences we may produce unique and widely divergent views. Two minds may have, for instance, different ontologies, both perhaps logically coherent and suitable to their respective purposes. The logical principals by which these two minds combed and tested their ontology may be identical.

3. More on types vs. particulars in relation to (2)."I would want to see some examples to illustrate the important relevance of types/ sets and particulars/members to (2)... I think you have a sense that types/sets are something more than 'more generalized thinking than a unitary identification of a specific object'."

(then you deliver, presciently...)

"Taking road (3), on types vs. particulars.

Suppose two computers A and B share software S.

S can exist without A, since if A were destroyed, S would still exist in B.

Same in the other direction: if B were destroyed, then S would exist in A.

So S doesn't depend locally on A, and S doesn't depend locally on B.

What is true for software is also true for logical consistency."

Both A and B are logically consistent.

"So they share logical consistency in common."

Yes, and the software still doesn't exist without the computers... And they do not 'share' logical consistency, they each independently exhibit it. Logical consistency it an accomplishment of a mind. Just like ballerinas demonstrate their own jetés , and don't share 'one jeté', and there is no 'jeté' as such, except when ballerinas are doing the actual jumping around.... It is only you who wants to define/declare the set to which you add these two computers. 'Similarity/sharing' is not of/by them. They are each utterly separate and independent. They are not changed by the others' existence or non-existence, nor by your labelling, grouping them conceptually into your current definition of 'sameness'. The objects share nothing, and not even do the two images of them you are manipulating in your mind. The 'sharing' is only that the two conceived computers in your mind further bear identical labels of 'member of Josh's set of identically configured Acer notebooks', also/only in your mind.

"Again, logical consistency -- the type -- is not the same as any token/particular logical consistency."

And the instance of S on computer A may be identical to one that is on computer B, but not the same instance. These instances can be distinguished by their locations as different even though similar in any other criterion. And this distinction is no different for the software than it is for any datum or bit the software manipulates, so there is no existential difference between type and element. They are different, but I am not hearing an articulation of the importance of their difference. Either can exist before/without the other.

"I hope these thoughts serve your system, or at least thoughts "similar" to mine. :)"

Yep. we're mutually debugging our versions of S, some of which we were shipped with, some of which we hacked on our own."

Josh:

"And they do not 'share' logical consistency, they each independently exhibit it. "

We return to the definition of "similar". Like I said, I don't understand "x is similar to y" except in terms of sharing something in common. Now you say, "they do not share S in common" (where S is logical consistency). In that case, I don't understand what it means to say they are similar. Nor do I understand what it means to say that they each independently exhibit it. If two things exhibit something, then that means there is something they exhibit. This something is not one and the same as the things that exhibit it. It is something else. We can call it "'more generalized thinking than a unitary identification of a specific object". That's fine. Call it anything. My thought, still, is that this something -- whatever we call it and however we analyze it -- is not the same as the particulars. It is a type.

Now you'll say the type is itself mental. I agree. We've agreed on that from the beginning.

What's at issue is whether there is anything individual things share in common. I say there is. My reason is that otherwise I don't *even know what it *means* to say individual things are similar in some respect.*

These are deep waters. A book that helps make the logical distinctions in play is Morelands' Universals. That book, together with Loux's Metaphysics to Metaphysics, helped me understand the logic of types. I recommend both. They will serve your system.

Joe:

"We return to the definition of "similar". Like I said, I don't understand "x is similar to y" except in terms of sharing something in common."

You first choose to recognize certain criteria as relevant, and decide that two objects each independently exhibit those criteria, then they share something you assign to them, membership in your set/type. It is your one type definition, but all else in their independent details of the members is currently irrelevant to you, and indeed there may be nothing in any of their independent details that anyone else would consider similar, and indeed these similar or non-similar things may have no existence whatever except as/because they exist in your mind.

"Now you say, "they do not share S in common" (where S is logical consistency). In that case, I don't understand what it means to say they are similar."

As above, they are similar as deemed by you, as per your chosen criteria. Each is logically consistent, and if one says 2+2=4, and the other says shows the process of solving two equations with two unknowns, we may deem that both exhibit logical consistency even though neither may have employed the same logical tests/disciplines to achieve logical integrity. The two ballerinas ' identically'/'similarly' avoided falling on their faces by exercising some subset of the leg and core and arm muscles, in perhaps different degrees and proportions according to the traction and conditions etc.

The ballerinas and two minds products are connected in no way when you're not comparing them, connecting them.

"Nor do I understand what it means to say that they each independently exhibit it. If two things exhibit something, then that means there is something they exhibit."

It means that they exhibit separate instances of the same class/ type.

"This something is not one and the same as the things that exhibit it."

Of course. Your mom and my mom exhibit pie-making. Pie is trivially not the same thing as mom or baking. My mom's pie is also independent of your mom's pie. You or I may decide to define a set/type 'pie' and assign those all those pies with the same label/identity (at least till you might taste my mom's pie ;)).

"It is something else. We can call it "more generalized thinking than a unitary identification of a specific object". That's fine. Call it anything. My thought, still, is that this something -- whatever we call it and however we analyze it -- is not the same as the particulars. It is a type."

Well, sure. This is elementary basic set building, generalizing based on chosen criteria. And there is no inherent hierarchy or order between instances and any set definition that defines their generalization. In some cases we are first aware of, and operate with specific instances, and later come to conceive/create the set definition by which we link them as instances of our specific generalization. In some other cases we first conceive of a general definition for a set, and only then proceed to find (or not) and use specific instances/members. Generalization is a fundamental tool of a mind's organizational arsenal.

"Now you'll say the type is itself mental. I agree. We've agreed on that from the beginning."

Good, absolutely. Categorization is an individual exercise in selectively choosing to highlight certain criteria and to ignore others. It is also a fluctuating effort, context-dependent on which criteria are important, when.

"What's at issue is whether there is anything individual things share in common. I say there is. My reason is that other wise I don't even know what it *means* to say individual things are similar in some respect."

I say there is too, but not intrinsically, only when you want to know/declare that individual things are similar. There is no 'sharing' between the objects themselves when we're not looking/comparing... It is us who associate them, who place them in common. We may come to agree that even though your and my mom's pies look identical and have the same ingredients and process, and that most of the sentient world would link them as in common when they consider them, you and I, the chosen few who tasted them both might be quite militant in adding or highlighting implicit or new criteria for anything to be allowed the label 'pie'. and that my mom's creations don't cut it. But even if the pies are identical in taste, texture, and any other criteria you choose, they don't intrinsically share anything, they are exactly and completely separate things. What we anoint them with, our concepts of them, is an identical symbol/label which indicates 'pie', the set of all objects/concepts we've given a label 'pie'. 'Pie' is a set, like a club. My membership in the club is not your membership in the club. We do not share a membership in the club. We each have our own identical badge. The existence or non-existence of the set/club does not per se affect either of us, nor does my membership or non-membership affect you or your membership. Everything intrinsic to a thing is intrinsic to it alone. Copies don't count, nor do labels (when we're creating them and doling them out), because each thing gets its own copy of the label(s) we may give it.

"These are deep waters."

We are swimmers. We don't drown as the water gets deeper. In fact we know there is much less land than others assume. In fact there is no reliable land you don't build on your own, and bring with you.

Josh:

"there is no reliable land you don't build on your own, and bring with you. "

I love that quote.

The next step comes into view with a question: what does a true thought about similarity correspond to? Suppose one has a true thought T that X and Y are similar with respect to Z. Since this thought is true, it corresponds with some reality R. What is R? Whatever it is, it is not the same as T, because T is the thought that corresponds to R. Put differently, R is the truth-maker for T. We can describe R this way: R is the state of X and Y being similar with respect to R. That is, R is a state of similarity.

Why is this significant? Because it shows that there's a difference between a state of similarity (like R) and a true thought about that state. The thought about similarity is true if that state of similarity is real. The state of similarity is the truth-maker, and the thought about similarity is the truth.

To illustrate, your thought of the LOI (law of identity) is similar to my thought of LOI. This state of similarity is real and is the truth-maker for your thought that they are similar. In other words, if you think those things are similar, then this thought is true if it corresponds to reality. What reality is that? Call it R. Whatever it is, R exists prior to your thought of it, just as a universe exists prior to your thoughts about the universe.

And a twig snaps beneath our feet.

Joe:

"The next step comes into view with a question: what does a true thought about similarity correspond to?"

A thought about similarity is, I would say, a thought which assumes/defines the qualities/aspects of an object by which it will be characterized as similar or not. And then the thought is about comparing objects to see whether they have those same qualities. I am not sure what a true thought would be, as opposed to a false thought about similarity... It would depend on the details of the thought. A basic declaration of similarity starts with declaring the relevant criteria. So far, this is a free construction, and has no truth value, it just is, unless there is logical incoherence between the criteria, such as 'a member must be blue', and 'a member cannot be blue', etc. This so far does not declare or identify that/whether there are any members of the defined set. A true statement about the/a similarity might be in declaring that certain things are members, or not. The truth would be based on the correct perception of the relevant criteria in the objects, and a false one would be mistaken in that regard.

"Suppose one has a true thought T that X and Y are similar with respect to Z."

Good. Z represents the current/relevant classification criteria, and we have correctly determined that X and Y have (identically, though independently) the required criteria. We have thusly given our concepts of X and Y, each their own copy of the label which indicates membership in Z.

"Since this thought is true,"

Let's work with two examples, one 'true', and one 'false':

Thought T: "This person A, and this person B each have the same relevant criteria, of being white male republicans. They are, according to these salient criteria, similar.

Thought F: (identical to T, except, the comparer has incorrect data, and person B does not meet one or more of the criteria.) or

Thought T2: "This person A and this person B are both white male republicans but one is gay so they are completely different."

(a claim of similarity/non-similarity are equally apt for this conversation) *"it (T) corresponds with some reality R. What is R? Whatever it is, it is not the same as T, because T is the thought that corresponds to R."*

The true thought T represents only a subjective reality that is entirely manifested when we are considering our conceptual construction Z, and its members. There is no other needed/relevant reality R, and indeed the R as defined does not exist, nor need it, as soon as we stop thinking about Z and it's members. All we need/have is the T as/when the comparer is defining/wielding the concept of the set Z by which the comparer unites the elements.

"Put differently, R is the truth-maker for T. We can describe R this way: R is the state of X and Y being similar with respect to R. That is, R is a state of similarity."

Reality R is more than a state of similarity. It comprises a set definition Z, and the correctly, relevantly conceived/identified/created objects X and Y which have then duly anointed, each with their own tramp-stamp tattoo of 'Z'. It is only you or I, the active comparer, with a created set/criteria Z that defines/creates similarity. Two cubes of iron share *nothing* physically, not location, not any atom in common, and they do not communicate etc. Neither of them is affected by the existence or non-existence of the other, or our conception of them as members of a set, or of the existence of a sphere of aluminum which someone else defines as similar to the two cubes, by their own different criteria for 'similar'. Similarity, like beauty, is only in the eyes of the comparer. Again, like before, two oxygen molecules can be deemed identical or vastly different, even according to the fantastical aesthetic overlays placed on them by 'poetic' viewers.

"Why is this significant? Because it shows that there's a difference between a state of similarity (like R) and a true thought about that state."

Hmmmm... The fact that *any* thought about anything is not the same as the thing, is general, and should be uncontroversial to us. I think I have successfully dispelled the idea that a 'state of similarity' though, exists in any way except in the mind of the comparer. If there is an objective realm, we posit with confidence that there is an R, an objective reality, in whole extant independent of any assertions about it, true or false. It is 'the state' of objective reality. And if we do not posit an objective reality, there is still one reality, your isolated, private, personal subjective reality, and as/if you compare one idea/vision/mental object with another, they themselves, just are, when/if they are, and are harmlessly non-existent, a given Z, X and Y, when you are not thinking of them.

"To illustrate, your thought of the LOI (law of identity) is similar to my thought of LOI."

Yes, we declare so, based on our trust in comparing our language for the law etc.

"This state of similarity is real and is the truth-maker for your thought that they are similar."

Not real unless:

1 - I am real independently of you, and vice versa etc.
2 – You and/or I are actively considering and equating our copies of LOI.
And more importantly for this conversation, not real, but rather, the similarity is true, to me, and independently true to you, according to our individual and hopefully matching criteria. Similarity is a proposition, not an attribute of reality per se. Reality itself needs no unification/classification. Those are only optional aims of the modeler of reality.

"In other words, if you think those things are similar, then this thought is true if it corresponds to reality."

Yes, according to your criteria for comparisons. But reality just *is*. Similarity is a mental construct, an assertion about reality, as categorized and differentiated/compared. There could be a case where one person says "A is similar to B" for whatever reasons, but some other person differs in their basic classification of reality does not have any way to distinguish A from B at all. As above, the objects themselves are a separate reality from a reality which includes a set definition which unites them. The reality in which a similarity Z is defined, is a conscious one, and even there Z may come and go, and Z may never be perceived (and therefor never exist) in a mind.

"What reality is that? Call it R. Whatever it is, R exists prior to your thought of it, just as a universe exists prior to your thoughts about the universe."

No. If this reality includes a 'similarity' such as Z, then this reality *is*, exists, only in your thoughts. Your determined/defined similarities/classifications/thoughts are only yours. Any objective reality R does not generate/contain similes.

"And a twig snaps beneath our feet."

Yes. I think we are stepping along, having snapped the twig that tried to project similarity as an aspect of reality, rather than what it is, a temporal and personal effort of classification."

Josh:

"I think I have successfully dispelled the idea that a 'state of similarity' though, exists in any way except in the mind of the comparer. "

Well, it is part of science that some ants have some features in common with spiders. Is this not true? For more on this argument from science, see "A Theory of Properties.".

If there is not state of similarity, then nothing has anything in common. Yet, many different statements are true. They have truth in common. Don't you agree? If not, I think we've reached a first principle. If you want me to argue for this principle, it's like trying to argue for my own existence or for the reality of my thoughts. I can try, but I think simply see directly that I exist, that I have thoughts, and that many statements are true. So I'm at the bottom of my mind!"

"Ultimately, there is no such thing as a property except as defined and discerned/theorized by an observer/considerer."

A form of Nominalism. I offer two sources to serve your inquiry. First, there is Peter van Inwagen's "A Theory of Properties" (which I mentioned last time). Second, there is J.P. Moreland's book, Universals.

I would be happy to consider any questions you may have about the arguments in those pieces.

Joe:

It doesn't seem to be nominalism exactly. There is practically infinite real 'properties' (parsable aspects) of the universe, and even for most of the smallest sub-divisions we see/agree on, such as atoms. I am just saying that the properties/qualities *we perceive and manipulate them in our minds* are mental constructs, hoped-to-be-accurate metaphors. The moon can be sub-divided into aspects/properties for your consideration, but it does not have these properties in a discrete pile locked in a hope chest, to lose or add one occasionally. The box and its discrete contents *are* named instances of qualities we assign/perceive/believe the moon to have. It is not that the moon is simpler, nor that the qualities (generalizations) are false. My point is that the moon, more complex in its parsibility than we can ever grasp, is nevertheless by itself unitary as an object. Nominalism would fail in its implication that there is no relationship between ideas/generalizations and reality, based on the inexorable and stunning predictive power of physics. The moon is like other natural satellites of other planets, and this claim is justified/supported to the degree of predictability of our definition of 'like' in this model. The moon's mass and velocity vector are valuable and well-parsed, fungible qualities of the moon, but such qualities are not independently extant/alterable in reality. One will instantly and proportionately change if the other does. Reality *is*, a whole. The issue is of our *understanding* of what reality is that requires parsing, generalizations, simplifications, and qualities (set membership criteria).

Josh:

"set membership criteria." Right, sometimes called "class-nominalism." But yes, I get it: you are saying properties are mental constructs. This is well-trodden terrain. I do think those references will you serve you in the examination of that view and its challenges.

(Again, feel free to send me any questions you may have about those sources.)

Best,

Josh

Joe:

I want to know if there's anything you disagree with, or don't understand, and why. The key is in the pristine, eternal and utter separation between the subjective and the objective. The 'biological intent'/value of the artificial/imaginary space-time is to model the objective world in practically profitable ways, but the model, however accurate, and whatever linguistic/conceptual building blocks there are in the creation of the model, remain only artifacts of that mental space. The objective space-time, by definition and seemingly actual, is utterly independent of, pre and post the existence of any subjectivity/mind.

Josh:

Your thinking is in your mind, but it isn't all of your mind.

I do hope you recover stronger than ever. I'm sorry about your struggle and challenge. You work is valuable. Get your book done!
:)

Here's a test case to consider:

1. Truth is not relative.

2. If attributes depends on your thinking of them, then truth is relative (e.g., the attribute of being true depends on your thinking of it).

3. Therefore, attributes don't depend on your thinking of them.

Why think truth is not relative? Well, because the alternative is self-defeating. Anyone who thinks truth is relative thinks it is true that truth is relative. They think, then, that those who accept (1) are mistaken. Yet, if truth is relative, then those who accept (1) are not mistaken. Instead, (1) is true relative to them.

The problem is even deeper. If truth is relative, there is no disagreement about anything. Everyone has their own truth. I can't say your truth is wrong because I don't even have your truth. Similarly, you can't say my truth is wrong because you don't have my truth. You and I cannot disagree about something unless there is something we disagree about. Yet, there is nothing we disagree about if there is nothing in common (like truth) between anything we ever think about.

Besides all of this, Peter van Inwagen shows (decisively in my view) that ordinary scientific claims logically entail that there are properties prior to one's grasp of them.

A key: thoughts in you are not thereby of you.

Joe:

"Here's a test case to consider:

Truth is not relative."

I disagree. The relativity of truth is first and inexorably tied to the subject of the specific truth (a given true assertion). 'Truth' is nothing more or less than the collection of all true statements. Truth depends on a mind expressing the/a truth, and does not exist, need not exist otherwise. If there is an objective reality, it just *is*, a-priori, independent of anyone that would make claims about it. Truths about the objective realm reside still and only in the conscious minds that assert them, *when* they assert them. Truths about the subjective realm are dependent *only* on the specific consciousness making the claim, and can be as evanescent in their truth as the changing opinion the claimer has on eggs between his first and thirtieth of the day. Yet at each instance it is true when uttered.

"2. If attributes depend on your thinking of them, then truth is relative (e.g., the attribute of being true depends on your thinking of it). "

Well, to be exact, it is the existence of a proposing mind on which a proposition, true or false depends on in order to exist as such, and the truth/falsity of a proposition does depend on the proposition's existing. And we should note that 'relative' is not a blanket mishmash of everything. An instance of relativity is a specific relationship between specific elements. As above, truth is always relative to one or more things. Yes, we've long passed agreement that a true proposition (as does a false proposition) depends first on its being proposed by the mind proposing it. Truth and falsity are symmetrical/identical in this dependence. But it is not that 'being true' is specifically/uniquely dependent on your thinking the proposition, and more/less than its being false.

"3. Therefore, attributes don't depend on your thinking of them."

False per the clarified failure of (1) and (2). Attributes are chosen conceptual 'cuts', 'facets', 'dimensions', constructed, narrowed generalizations of a more complex entity/concept. For example, we could define the attribute of kindness is a narrowly defined behavior/attitude which conscious beings may have or not have, and which inanimate objects cannot. This attribute does not, need not exist except as/when we observe behavior and judge whether it evidences kindness. The behavior per se, unexamined, is separate from any label we might apply to it.

"Why think truth is not relative? Well, because the alternative is self-defeating. Anyone who thinks truth is relative thinks it is true that truth is relative. They think, then, that those who accept (1) are mistaken. Yet, if truth is relative, then those who accept (1) are not mistaken. Instead, (1) is true relative to them."

No, per my response to (1). All truth is relative to the subject of the truth, and even for truths about objective subjects, the truth is still relative to the truth-speaker. Even if you and I agree that '2+2=4', our identical assertions of this depend necessarily on our own private conceptions of cardinality, numbers etc, none of which have mind-independent existence. Truth is relative to (extant only because of) the asserter of the correct assertion(s), as well as being relative specifically to the aspect of reality they describe. Some of such truths can importantly be mind-in-variant, such as the whole body of pure mathematics, but they remain mind-dependent, which can be said to mean relative to the mind. And yes, there are certainly bodies of truths whose truth values are relative to the specific asserter because the truths are *about* the asserter. "It is cold in this room!" is, if correctly understood by the asserter and listeners, to mean it is cold to the asserter, and that anyone else is free to assert the same or differently about that room, in their opinion/experience.

"The problem is even deeper. If truth is relative, there is no disagreement about anything."

Not true. Again, relativity depends, narrowly and specifically on the specific subject of a given truth. I promise you that when my wife and I are in the same room together, we can disagree on whether it is warm or cold. :) Our truths in that case are relative to our individual experience, as well as the neutral objective temperature of the room. And for our arguments about how many cheetos I left in the bag, she or I can be wrong, but the truth is relative to the objective content/condition of the bag, as well as our both existing and making our competing propositions. We each have our truths, and we can easily agree/disagree that/when our truths are semantically identical/different/opposite.

"Everyone has their own truth."

Yes, everyone has their own collection of that they believe to be true statements/images. Sometimes I sit am content to passively have no truths on the fire at all.

"I can't say your truth is wrong because I don't even have your truth."

Yes you can, as I described between my wife and me. Yes, you never have my truth, but we can discern whether your truth is semantically identical to mine. You can say my assertion is wrong or right if we agree that the topic of the assertion/truth is objective or at least mind-invariant. Math and logic are full of this ability. You can perfectly reason/support that my '2+2=4' is true, as is your '2+2=4', and you can perfectly reject my assertion that '2+2=3'.

"Similarly, you can't say my truth is wrong because you don't have my truth."

Wrong. (I crack myself up!) Again, if the topic of the truth is mind-invariant, it can be logically provable, even axiomatic, or it can be provably false for any mind. If your 'truth' is "2+2=5", then I can say, and prove it wrong.

"You and I cannot disagree about something unless there is something we disagree about. Yet, there is nothing we disagree about if

there is nothing in common (like truth) between anything we ever think about."

What we have in common is:

1 - the objective environment we occupy.

2 - the strictures and limitations we accept in order to demand/maintain logical coherency of our self.

As previous, we each have our set of assertions. If we come to find that you have a semantically identical assertion, we can have a common agreement on the truth-values of our respective copies.

"Besides all of this, Peter van Inwagen shows (decisively in my view) that ordinary scientific claims logically entail that there are properties prior to one's grasp of them."

I hear that you are convinced, and I ask you to help distinguish that credulity as logically, linguistically integrated proof, and not a 'seems true' feeling. Scientific claims are based on the supposition of an objective realm, and are only supported statistically, never provable. Ordinary mathematical/logical claims do not entail that there are any 'properties' or even objects, except as defined/used in the given claim. I define properties as point generalizations, as I exemplified previously with 'kindness'. Hardness, length, temperature etc. are no different as considered and used to judge objects in scientific' claims. Length per se, does not and need not, and cannot exist except as declared/defined by a would-be measurer.

167

"A key: thoughts in you are not thereby of you."

I disagree. Your every thought is of/by you, your sole and private construction, as are mine to me. Show me a counter-example. And your usage of 'of you' seems to refer to the topic of my/your thoughts, and most of them are not about me/you but some are, All the Shakespeare, academic texts etc contain nothing, no thoughts. They intend to symbolize the authors thoughts, but no such actual thoughts exist, until/unless you privately and personally parse and construct your own living thoughts/interpretations as to what the authors meant. Ideally, hopefully your thoughts that are evoked by your interpreting the language of Shakespeare come close to being semantically, aesthetically close to the authors originals.

Josh:

My thought of you is not of me. :)

This email contained nothing until you read it. Wait, no, it contained something as soon as I typed it! :)

If all truth is purely relative, then it is true relative to me that truth is not relative. Is that true?

Best.

Joe:

"This email contained nothing until you read it. Wait, no, it contained something as soon as I typed it! :) "

No, the meaning remained in your mind, the specific associations you made between the symbols you typed and the meanings you held for them. Our emails are examples of our shared symbology, but symbols don't have intrinsic meaning. They only 'have meaning' by specific association and retrieval of that meaning, residing as a living concept, in the mind of the retriever, who associated the symbol with the meaning. And what they mean is first only as clear as the intended meaning of the author, but when/while commissioned to the internet deep, they mean nothing, they just are, bits, which may or may not be taken as symbols, but only ever by a consciousness who also wields the requisite symbology and hopefully identical meanings to draw on in order to create/ enact the intended experience. When the recipient translates/ relates each symbol to the actual live in-his-mind meaning of the symbol, and constructs the composite meaning, then there is a second, ideally identical meaning/experience/imagery made at that end.

" If they are properties we have in common, then the door is open to things sharing properties in common. If the sharing of properties in common depends first on your thought of this sharing, then the truth of a thought is not a matter of correspondence with some prior reality. Seeing this is valuable. It is a form of progress to see clearly the connection between the view you've articulated and relative truth.

If all truth is purely relative, then it is true relative to me that truth is not relative. Is that true?"

OK, yes, strictures... They are identical, but individual. Your constitutional pre-analytic revulsion to someone contradicting themselves within one run-on sentence is perhaps like mine, but like our balance, we wield only our own. Not sharing exactly, but mirroring, harmonizing. Consciousness is never a party line. You and I each have our own '2's and "+'s to wield.

I see where we can break through to the next step, when you say 'purely relative', as if this is a diminishment. Again, relativity does not imply variability, capriciousness, or free association etc. Truth is *meta*. It is *about* something, it is not reality itself. Truth is a relation between (relative to) the observer and the specific aspect of reality which a given truth addresses. If a particular truth is about some aspect of the objective world, then this truth will be the *same* for all who assert it. It's obverse will symmetrically be a falsehood for all who assert that.

The relativity of truth/falsehood is more complex and pointed than meaning that 'the truth value of any assertion depends only on the asserter'. *Some truths* are such, many are not. Nevertheless, each truth is a tiny narrowed-view chip of the holograph which is the model of reality constructed in the mind of the asserter.

Josh:

"Truth is a relation between the observer and reality."

Yes, we agree on this.

"If a particular truth is about some aspect of the objective world, then this truth will be the *same* for all who assert it."

I don't know what "it" is supposed to refer to. Are you talking about a property in your own mind that isn't also in my mind? If so, then I have no idea what that property is.

"It's obverse will symmetrically be a falsehood for all who assert that.

The relativity of truth/falsehood is more complex and pointed than meaning that 'the truth value of any assertion depends only on the asserter'. *Some truths* are such, many are not. Nevertheless, each truth is a tiny narrowed-view chip of the holograph which is the model of reality constructed in the mind of the asserter."

Just to clarify, we can distinguish between the thing that is true (e.g., the proposition that 2+2=4) and the property, being true. On your account, both depend on the one who thinks of the truth in question. For example, <2+2=4> is only true if you have a certain thought or concept. On my view your thought that 2+2=4 would be true even if you didn't even have any concept of truth. It would *be true simply by corresponding with reality (a reality we agree is a mental reality).*

Josh"

Joe:

"" The argument I gave before was about all the property, true. That very property is relative, on your view, since it is a mental construct in your mind. I don't have that same property in my mind, on your view. The very property is relative. "

OK, we can talk about the property/quality/categorization that is called 'true'. Of course it's relative, in that it relates the proposition with the reality the proposition intends to illustrate/mirror. 'True' is a set, along with 'false'. These two disjoint sets contain all propositions.

We can further divide each of those sets into two, the set of propositions about the objective realm, and the set of propositions about the subjective realm (that of the persons' mind).

Your set of true or false statements will necessarily differ from mine, at the basic level that they each depend on your or my asserting each one, and we may asserting other things, or at times nothing at all etc, and even when we agree, it is the functional/semantic similarity of your assertion with mine. In other words, all truths and/or falsehoods as such, independent of their truth value, are relative to the asserter, the asserter's view/vision of reality.

But loosening one step, to where we can say that my "2+2=4" is semantically the same as your "2+2=4", the relativity of truths is lastly dependent on the subject of the truth. For truths/falsehoods about the subjective, those whose subject matter is some aspect about the asserter themself, including the constructs/visions/ideas in his head, the assertions are doubly/completely relative to the asserter, such as "I am cold". There is no necessary bond/connection/relation between that assertion and what someone else might say, even using the same terms/meanings. But I want to further divide this subjective set into those assertions about the asserter themself, and those assertions that are derived strictly by logical building from subjective axioms. This area is where we find mathematics and logic proofs etc, and this set, though subjective in the strictest sense because they are still assertions, requiring an asserter, produce mind-invariant truths. These truths can be called 'objective' in the second-level definition of 'objective' I describe, early in the book.

On the other side, those truths/falsehoods that assert about the objective realm, do 'share a bond' independent of the disparate asserters. Such truths/falsehoods, by virtue of their subject being objective (extant as-is, independent of any viewer/asserter) are all relative to the one objective reality. All 'objective truths' are about, bound to, tested against a single common reality, such that of competing assertions on a topic, only one at most will be true. In fact, because of the overwhelming complexity of macro-objective reality, and perhaps (I believe) the dunning simplicity as we get smaller in the micro-objective reality, our assertions may always be crude approximations, whose truths may be at best 'sufficient for the purpose'.

"If a particular truth is about some aspect of the objective world, then this truth will be the *same* for all who assert it.

I don't know what "it" is supposed to refer to. Are you talking about a property in your own mind that isn't also in my mind? If so, then I have no idea what that property is."

An example of 'it', an assertion about the objective world, is "The moon is comprised of green cheese". The truth value of this assertion, whoever makes it, is governed by the one objective reality. In this case, the assertion will be false for all who assert it. I may not be understanding your not-understanding... Or did I clear myself up?

"Just to clarify, we can distinguish between the thing that is true (e.g., the proposition that 2+2=4) and the property, being true."

Yes, absolutely. As above, 'being true', membership in that subset of propositions, is the condition that a proposition correctly models/mirrors the aspect of reality (whether subjective or objective) it addresses. '2+2=4' is just one example.

"On your account, both depend on the one who thinks of the truth in question."

Well, the definition of the 'true set' would seemingly be a trivially agreed-on consensus, and is not an assertion as such. The so-defined set might be empty etc. But yes, your set of assertions true and/or false are still *your* assertions, and depend therefore on you, fundamentally for their existence, without regard and a-priori to their truth values. But also, at a practical level, to be tested occasionally, we can verify/trust that many/all of our mind-invariant truths can be used to construct more mind-invariant truths we can share(copy and understand).

"For example, <2+2=4> is only true if you have a certain thought or concept."

Well, it is true, if and only if it is an assertion, and it is only an assertion if you assert/entertain it. Nothing is true or false to/in/for you when you're out like a carp at 3AM. For you, '2', '+', etc don't exist as such, and need not, when you're not actively conceiving them, usually in a more complex assertion you're making, such as '2+2=4'.

"On my view your thought that 2+2=4 would be true even if you didn't even have any concept of truth. It would be true simply by corresponding with reality (a reality we agree is a mental reality)."

Would be true'? You and I agree that the successful wielding of logic will invariantly derive the assertion that 2+2=4. But this eminently mind-invariant assertion does not *exist*, *need* not exist, except as/when asserted, and existence is a-priori to, and independent of which side of the truth/falsity fence it will fall to.

'Would be true' is a prediction you're making (at the time you typed that) of mind-invariance, over time and over minds, and I agree about 2+2=4, but exactingly, that assertion is only true when it exists. That mental reality only exists when you're awake.

Everyone has a concept of truth, if only that everyone has a world-view which he takes mostly unquestioningly as mirroring, even *being* reality. It takes a next step of sophistication to divide into truth vs. falsehood, typically after one has found themselves misled enough times by their visions...

Much thanks,

Joe

Joe:

Some truths are governed by the one objective reality (the body of physics, for example). But as any assertion, any truth/falsity is relative to the asserter. It is his/her assertion. Some truths are doubly (more deeply) relative to the asserted because their subject is the asserter. "I exist" is utterly subjective, and axiomatic. It is true whenever uttered.

'Relative', I would define generically, neutrally, simply and semantically mechanistically, as 'related to, dependent in some way with'. First, a statement is relative to, depends on the stater, in order that it exist, and statements *only* function/exist as such, in that living context. A second aspect of a statement is its truth value, which is secondary to the existence of the statement, and may not be known or knowable, or may be provable or even axiomatic, truly logically undoubtable. That aspect of an assertion, true or false is (specifically and hopefully obviously) relative to the specific subject/topic of the assertion.

So tell me what your intent/definition of 'relative' is, and we can either converge, or decide which of our competing and clear definitions of 'relative' will stand, and we'll create a second term for the other definition! :) "

Josh:

Hi Joe! I'm doing well, thanks. I hope you are doing well. How is your health, if I may ask?

"*Some* truths are governed by the one objective reality (the body of physics, for example). But as any assertion, any truth/falsity is relative to the asserter. It is his/her assertion. Some truths are doubly (more deeply) relative to the asserted because their subject is the asserter. "I exist" is utterly subjective, and axiomatic. It is true whenever uttered. "

True. :)

"'Relative', I would define generically, neutrally, simply and semantically mechanistically, as 'related to, dependent in some way with'. First, a statement is relative to, depends on the stater, in order that it exist, and statements *only* function/exist as such, in that context. A second aspect of a statement is its truth value, which is secondary to the existence of the statement, and may not be known or knowable, or may be provable or even axiomatic, truly logically undoubtable.

So tell me what your intent/definition of 'relative' is, and we can either converge, or decide which of our competing and clear definitions of 'relative' will stand, and we'll create a second term for the other definition! :)"

Makes sense, as far as I can tell.

We've gone around on this topic for a while. When I step back to see the big picture, it looks to me that you are rightly seeing that propositions are conceptual realities. Truths are also conceptual, because a truth is a proposition that is true.

My point in our conversation has been to separate the above insight from the furthers questions about the conceptual reality. In particular, do any propositions you see within your mind exist even while you are not seeing them? For example, do principles of logic hold even while you are not entertaining those principles? I think so. As we discussed, I think that makes the best sense of (i) how the same logic can be shared across cultures and languages, (ii) the sense that logic couldn't be otherwise, and (iii) the truth-maker for true logical thoughts. As with anything, there is room for reasonable disagreement and further inquiry.

I appreciate this conversation, your inquiry, and your work. I look forward to your book. :)

Best, Josh

Joe:

Hi, Absolutely no concepts/assertions/propositions exist except as/when actually/currently conceived/asserted/proposed by a given conceiver/asserter/proposer. There is no need nor logical possibility of otherwise. The mind is *the* required context for any such thing to exist, and any such thing is not in evidence nor effect except as it actively functions when in the mind. The fact that some propositions are mind-invariant, freely, identically, and independently derivable by any mind which manifests sufficient logic to coherently concatenate the derivation is in no way indicative of anything more permanent than a mind and what it can make and remember. And there is no representation, evidence, or even definition of a proposition *as such*, pre, post, or absent a proposer. The principals of logic are just propositions. They don't 'hold' except as/when evidenced and affirmed in the judgment of a(any) logical argument. This is exactly like there is no balance, let alone the need for the principals of balance, except when/where there is someone/something balancing. Nothing 'holds'. Nothing holds except as/when someone is holding it. There is room for reasonable disagreement, only until we get sharp enough that one reasonable side is unable to counter the others position.

We come up with similar answers to some classes of questions precisely because they are in a field/realm where being self-consistent among ones own ideas is all that is necessary to arrive at those answers. We start with largely identical 'hardware', our mind, with its ability to symbolize, generalize, and equate etc, though each of us is a different instance of such. I vigorously reject the 'one mind' metaphor. Each mind is private, a singular focus. And even for the subjects for which we generally come up with identical answers, *some* of us still get it wrong, and still others of us never find/ask those questions at all. But clearest, from the subjective perspective, the 'hardware' is simple, individual logical self-consistency when considering a connected string of thoughts. No external/social/'transcendent' dependency is needed or possible. Logic is just *self* consistency.

'Principles of logic' are just assertions like any others, and do not/need not/cannot exist except in a mind. They are a collection of axioms (assertions which are undoubtable, true whenever asserted) and some few basic but more complex assertions built from those axioms. Logic, as a created conceptual framework, is simply thoughts about thoughts, and exists only as/when logicians are operating. Logic as more simply, commonly *demonstrated*, is just an act/accomplishment of a given instance of coherent thoughts, by one, judged so by a viewer (who may be the same individual). Again as I've said before, logic can be analogized like balance to a gymnast. The gymnast may exhibit balance, or exhibit a failure of balance in their acts, but there is no balance, there need be no balance, there can be no balance as such, when no one is doing anything. The same is true of logic or thoughts in general. There is not, need not, and cannot be thoughts, or any discipline/coherence between them, when there is no thinker, and I will aver that there are plenty of times when I am not a thinker, and still other times when I am at most charged with attempted logic. ;)

No thoughts, and no logic or illogic in their combinations, except when there are thinkers, and from an objective perspective, zero need for either. From a subjective perspective, the self is a-priori, necessary, uncaused, but no particular thought/image/assertion/concept exists except as/when the self(you) ponders it.

Josh:

"The mind is *the* required context for any such thing to exist, and any such thing is not in evidence nor effect except as it actively functions when in the mind."

Right, we've agreed on this from the beginning. Without mind, there is no logic.

The only remaining question is whether logic depends on your mind in order for you to know about it. Well, not everything you know about depends on your mind. The author of this email doesn't depend on your mind. Yet, you can still know -- or be reasonably sure -- that this email has an author.

So is there any reason or evidence for thinking logic depends on your mind?

We can give a scientific case against dependence. The case is about prediction. Logic-permanence successfully predicts three things: (i) that every time we check the logical principles, we see that the correct ones are still the same (this is also a consequence of standard S4 logic); (ii) our ability to translate the same logic across languages and individual human minds; (iii) that there is a difference between you false thoughts about logic and your correct thoughts about logic, where a correct thought is one that corresponds to -- or made true by -- an actual logical reality which your thought is about.

Is there a better way to account for those predictions?

"My best sense of how we come up with similar answers is that we start with identical 'hardware', though different instances of such."

By the transitivity of identity, the hardware H is not the same as its different instances. If instance A differs from B, then H cannot be one and the same as A and also one and the same as B. Indeed, H can exist without A, and H can exist without B. So H doesn't even depend on its instances. This observation fits perfectly with the logic-permanence hypothesis. Logic doesn't depend on every individual thought that thinks about it.

Again, we agree that logic cannot exist without a mind. The only question is whether logic has a permanent nature.

"I vigorously reject the 'one mind' metaphor. Each mind is private, a singular focus."

Right.

"And even for the subjects for which we generally come up with identical answers, *some* of us still get it wrong, and still others of us never find/ask those questions at all."

Yep.

"But clearest, from the subjective perspective, the 'hardware' is simple, individual logical self-consistency when considering a connected string of thoughts."

Agreed., as long as we distinguish the type of hardware from its individual instances.

"No external/social/'transcendent' dependency is needed or possible. Logic is just *self* consistency."

Yep, I'm with you. Logic depends on an individual mind. We've been in agreement on this point from the beginning. The only question is about the nature of this mind. My scientific argument above confirms that logic has a nature that no more depends on your mind than does the author of this email. If your system can take

into account that data, it will be beautiful and unusually powerful.
:)

"'Principles of logic' are just assertions like any others, and do not/need not/cannot exist except in a mind."

Agreed.

"They are a collection of axioms (assertions which are undoubtable, true whenever asserted) and some few basic but more complex assertions built from those axioms."

Yep.

"Logic, as a created conceptual framework, is simply thoughts about thoughts."

Was it logically possible to create a conceptual framework in which A and not A?

"Logic as *demonstrated*, is just an act/accomplishment by one, judged by a viewer (who may be the same individual). Again as I've said before, logic can be analogized like balance to a gymnast. The gymnast may exhibit balance, or exhibit a failure of balance in their acts, but there is no balance, there need be no balance, there can be no balance as such, when no one is doing anything. The same is true of logic or thoughts in general. There is not, need not, and cannot be thoughts, or any discipline/coherence between them, when there is no thinker, and I will aver that there are plenty of times when I am not a thinker, and still other times when I am at most charged with attempted logic. ;)"

I love your analogies!

"No thoughts, and no logic or illogic in their combinations, except when there are thinkers, and from an objective perspective, zero need for either. From a subjective perspective, the self is a-priori, necessary, uncaused, but no particular thought/image/assertion/ concept exists except as/when the self(you) ponders it."

I celebrate our agreement about the dependence of logic on mind. :)"

Joe:

"The only remaining question is whether logic depends on your mind in order for you to know about it. Well, not everything you know about depends on your mind. The author of this email doesn't depend on your mind. Yet, you can still know -- or be reasonably sure -- that this email has an author."

Well, yes, absolutely and trivially, logic or anything else you know, depends on your mind in order that you know it. You do not know about any external author except by your experience and inferences. You may infer that the author exists independently of you, but only after the author exists even as a hypothesis of yours. So, fundamentally nothing exists, from your perspective, except

185

as you know it, by direct deduction, experience and interpretation. And no other external reality exists, no other independent space-time where you could posit anything else's independent existence, exists except as a working leap of faith in your mind. We each, mostly make that leap, but the existence of that author is permanently more doubtable than '2+2=4' is for you, derivable always, whenever you are self consistent.

I should mention the two usages of the term 'logic'. One of them is the formal mathematical study/usage of written rules, axioms and syntax etc, in the formal proof/analysis of arguments. The other usage is in the not-necessarily-meta-analyzed assumption and exhibition of logical integrity in ones' thoughts. The former could be used to later formally approve of/verify the on-the-fly thoughts/assumptions that a being made in solving a current problem. The behavior/thoughts of the being in action reveal logic like the balance analogy I used previously. They simply 'do not fall'. The example of the puppy looking around the other side of the mirror for his new pal is humorous *because* of the correct logic we see them apply, albeit to erroneous premises.

So, that being said, *your* living logic is exactly and only dependent on *your* mind, just like your living balance is dependent exactly and only on your physical proprioception. Yes, everything you know is an image/proposition *in your mind*. You constructed it. It absolutely and only depends on your mind.

If there is anything besides/outside of your mind, such as that author, it is eternally a matter of faith, however reasonable or unreasonable your projection is on inductive/statistical grounds. And some others of some people's projections may be as deeply felt/held with very weak inductive/logical grounds... In a formal setting, we would compare/judge projections based on the quality and integration of the premises and logic applied.

"So is there any reason or evidence for thinking logic depends on your mind? "

There is rather no avoiding that conclusion. Again, logic is the self-consistency of your chain of thought. It depends on your living execution of thoughts, and nothing else. There is no reason for you, except for your mind. There is no evidence for you except for/in your mind. There is no thinking at all, logical or not, except for your mind. The eternally moot projection that there are other minds is unnecessary for defining or evidencing reason, logic, thinking etc.

"We can give a scientific case against dependence. The case is about prediction. Logic-permanence successfully predicts three things: (i) that every time we check the logical principles, we see that the correct ones are still the same (this is also a consequence of standard S4 logic); (ii) our ability to translate the same logic across languages and individual human minds; (iii) that there is a difference between you false thoughts about logic and your correct thoughts about logic, where a correct thought is one that corresponds to -- or made true by -- an actual logical reality which your thought is about."

(i) Every time we open the refrigerator door, the light is on. That does nothing to support the notion or need that the light is on when the door is shut, or that the conceptual refrigerator we're imagining exists when we forget about it. Mind-invariance is enough. Mind-independence is too much, unneeded, unwarranted, and impossible/incoherent. Just because you can derive the same answer every time you try, it does not support that the answer has any independent existence.

(ii) Having everyone on earth take a turn at opening the fridge door does not strengthen the argument. Our ability to translate/communicate logic etc is unsure/incomplete, and fails at times, because, at the most important reasons, the failure of logic on the part of one end or other of the attempted communication. Transmission depends on the exhibition/ability/'balance' of the individuals at each end, and their matching interpretation of symbols. Nothing outside of them, 'in the middle' matters except that it is one objective thing. It's all dead paper and ink in between. No matter how pristine the logic is in the author, and even if the symbology is perfectly shared, it is resolutely and solely the individual ability for logic in the reader that determines whether there is to be a successful reproduction of the author's thoughts in the reader.

(iii) Well, truths and falsities may exist, each with pristine logic but correct or incorrect premises respectively. But with correct premises, the difference between a derived true proposition and a derived false proposition is in your personal logical 'balance'/integrity. In the false case you simply fell, whether you know it yet or not. A formal logical analysis would reveal the fall. And just to make it as fun/complicated as real life, there can be a 'compensating' mix of incorrect premises and faulty logic that someone could have and combine to arrive nevertheless at a true proposition! This latter point is more important to human affairs/ survival than it might seem. If a tribe employs ultimately laughable imagery and utterly flaccid logic with magical threats and promises to arrive at directives that they support one another in society, that's all practically needed, and even today, except in august forums devoted to philosophy, it is better to be happy and right, than it is to have a world view and moral platform that are rigorously vetted from a logical integrity perspective. The only danger (and it is more ambient recently) is when there is social material change that 'uncompensates' the house-of-cards views that had given sufficient answers previously. It will only be logically sound views, with correct premises, that will survive all changes in application/circumstances. And the 'actual logical reality' you refer to, is a subjective reality in your mind, and implies no other reality.

"Is there a better way to account for those predictions?"

Yes, as above. If you have a mind that can obey "A=A", whether consciously or intuitively, for the length of a chain of arguments, and so do I, we will independently and duplicatively arrive at identical decisions. Nothing more needed, nothing other apparent, nor possible. I don't need any other mind, nor do you.

"By the transitivity of identity, the hardware H is not the same as its different instances. If instance A differs from B, then H cannot be one and the same as A and also one and the same as B. Indeed, H can exist without A, and H can exist without B. So H doesn't even depend on its instances. This observation fits perfectly with the logic-permanence hypothesis. Logic doesn't depend on every individual thought that thinks about it."

H is a generalization, a specification one can have in ones' mind for a type of hardware, and this spec, like the spec for a unicorn, can exist independent of whether instances exist. Indeed A and B can exist, and *be* identical, such that they would qualify as instances of H, without H existing. The only point is that independent instances of H, A and B, will behave the same. This does not support permanence of H in any way. H is still just a concept, and does not exist, need not exist, cannot exist except while being constructed/wielded in the mind of the generalist that assays, for instance that persons A and B act the same, in a given context, and so they will (or could) be categorized as instances of 'republican'... 'Republican' and H, if/when they exist, are just defined set, extant only in the mind. Persons A and B or computers A and B may have no interaction or mutual relevance at all for their whole lives. It is only the mind of the aggregator who defines his sets and populates them, whether or not A's and B's exist. And if the would-be aggregator does not aggregate, H and 'republican' don't exist, even if A's and B's do.

Logic depends on thoughts. A premise is a thought, but does not need logic. A conclusion, deduced by combining two premises depends on logic. Logic is an optional attribute of a chain of linked premises producing a conclusion. Logic is less frequent than general thoughts.

"Again, we agree that logic cannot exist without a mind. The only question is whether logic has a permanent nature."

The answer to the question, IMO, is there is no logic, nor need there be, nor can there be, other than as/when exhibited by a given mind. Zero permanence, exactly like there is no balance except when bodies are teetering successfully, whether or not others are falling. Everyone sleeping or falling? No balance. Everyone sleeping or no one extant? No balance or logic. One person awake? Are they inducing/deducing? no? no logic. yes? maybe. If he/she is self-consistent in his thoughts, they will/can derive 1+1=2. If they not, they may assert it's 3. Two persons awake? Same, independently for each.

"No external/social/'transcendent' dependency is needed or possible. Logic is just *self* consistency."

Yep, I'm with you. Logic depends on an individual mind. We've been in agreement on this point from the beginning. The only question is about the nature of this mind. My scientific argument above confirms that logic has a nature that no more depends on your mind than does the author of this email. If your system can take into account that data, it will be beautiful and unusually powerful. :)"

Let me know if I've convinced you otherwise yet. I think my system is as powerful as it's going to get. Its utility/shareability will increase as I include and sharpen more definitions, especially of words that are more squishy in common philosophic usage.

"Logic, as a created conceptual framework, is simply thoughts about thoughts. Was it logically possible to create a conceptual framework in which A and not A?"

It is certainly possible to imagine a framework where logic ultimately does not hold, just see 'communism' ;), but it is not possible to create a *logical* (self-consistent) conceptual framework that declares incongruity as a tenet.

"No thoughts, and no logic or illogic in their combinations, except when there are thinkers, and from an objective perspective, zero need for either. From a subjective perspective, the self is a-priori, necessary, uncaused, but no particular thought/image/assertion/concept exists except as/when the self(you) ponders it.

"I celebrate our agreement about the dependence of logic on mind. :) I hope you are doing well, my friend."

I *am*. I have seen an exponential increase in happiness between problem-solvers when they cross a certain critical mass of agreement. We may be near that.."

Josh:

I like your use of metaphors and imagery. I hope you are bringing those into your book. Also, do you have a writing schedule. I am looking forward to your book getting published! :) Just write a little every day, and you'll be surprised how quickly it finishes.

Btw, my book comes out today, How Reason Can Lead to God, https://www.ivpress.com/how-reason-can-lead-to-god. I would be honored for you to have it.

You offer a helpful distinction between two meanings of "logic". I wonder if we could think of it in terms of logic that is internal to a mind and logic that is also external to your particular mind. Then we could give a scientific case for transcendent logic, like the case for electrons. In both cases, we have a hypothesis that successfully predicts observations. The hypothesis of transcendent logic successfully predicts that every time you have a logical thought, you witness the same logical truths.

Best,

Josh

Joe:

Thanks.

I cannot see a way that there can be any meaning, purpose, or access to 'logic external to a mind'.

What is the 'like electrons' analogy?

There is no one central "if A = B and B = C then A = C" that we all tap into. We each grasp and/or manifest this (when/if we do) personally. Some get it, and some don't. Those that get it, constructed it on their own. We are each solitary. The seemingly clear reason (from an objective perspective) of our deriving identical proofs, identical equations is that:

1 - we are similar

2 - Logic, the desire/pursuit of self-consistency is based on the stricture/circumstance/desire of there being only one self (you, minimally), and one reality for you to view/model. You don't want to disagree with yourself, so you demand of yourself that you choose either 'A' or 'not A'. And this personal hygiene is absolutely optional, and by degree. We all know of some who are broadly or selectively willing to forego it, or unable to maintain it, for whatever personal reasons there are. Again, logic is self-consistency of ideas/images etc. The 'self' in self-consistency is a mind, and the only space-time/environment where ideas/images exist is in a mind. Nothing external to the mind is necessary or provable.

Logic is a predictable outcome of a unitary self, a self that desires/ sees a unitary reality. No other selves need to exist, let alone any externality to dictate what you will be, can be, will believe. Logic is about *you*. To expand on (1) "we are similar', all this similarity needs to be, is that we each are unitary, isolated, sovereign and wholly responsible to manifest (only ones' own) self-consistency.

Nothing else needed, nothing else simpler, and nothing else really possible. Nothing transcendent needed or possible. All that is needed/explanatory is the desired constancy of self. Just like an animal wants to maintain control over its physical position, it will maintain its balance in response to the particular inputs and physical circumstance it is in. We are all such animals, and we keep our own balance. Nothing transcendent actually needed for this self-developed skill, other than the individuals' desire to keep their physical integrity by not falling to their death. "

Josh:

"I cannot see a way that there can be any meaning, purpose, or access to 'logic external to a mind'.

Right, you and I agree that logic depends on a mind.

Or are you saying that you cannot see how to access a mind that is external to your own? Do you think I exist? How?

"What is the 'like electrons' analogy?"

Scientists posit electrons to explain their observations. Similarly, you can posit a mind (and logic) outside of your own mind to explain your observations.

"There is no one central "if A = B and B = C then A = C" that we all tap into."

I realize you think that. Question: why? Do you evidence? Would you say there are no electrons? No other minds? Electrons and minds explain your inner-experiences. So does universal logic.

"To expand on (1) "we are similar', all this similarity needs to be, is that we each are unitary, isolated, sovereign and wholly responsible to manifest (only ones' own) self-consistency. Nothing else needed, nothing else simpler, and nothing else really possible. Nothing transcendent needed or possible. "

Well, I already demonstrated that transcendent logic is needed at the start of this thread. The subsequent emails were about clarifying terms so you could understand the proof I provided. But here you say that nothing else is even possible. Maybe it would serve your system to provide a proof of the impossibility. That will help you make clear the underlying premises of your system. We both agree that logic depends on a mind. But how do you deduce that all the logic you access depends on your mind? If you could deduce that, you could become famous! I'm serious.

Best wishes,

Josh

Joe:

"Right, you and I agree that logic depends on a mind."

Good, and we only ever have direct, deducible access to our own mind, therein to wield only our own logic.

"Or are you saying that you cannot see how to access a mind that is external to your own? Do you think I exist? How?"

No, I have no practical doubt that the objective realm exists, and that you exist like I do, in a body imagining things in your mind, and that we've successfully co-opted some little bits of the mindless objective world between us to generate, send, receive and interpret symbols to convey meaning to one another. But this is eternally a matter of faith in my chain of projections and interpretations. I first presume that I am crudely and limitedly experiencing something of a real objective universe, via my senses. I then observe that some of the patterns I see, that I interpret as things, seem dead and inert, like rocks etc, where other 'things' seem animate and independently reactive, and further that they seem to react physically and seemingly emotionally to my gestures and sounds, quite as if they are like me, as if they have a mind of their own. I project (and statistically very successfully) that they are such, and we cooperate and communicate via symbols we seem to find easy to agree on, from gestures and sounds, evolving to symbols which start from crude marks and evolving to electronic missives at a distance. It is only via this chain of working-but-never-logically-provable presumptions, and our ongoing development of agreed-on symbolism that I posit my reaching other minds.

"Scientists posit electrons to explain their observations. Similarly, you can posit a mind (and logic) outside of your own mind to explain your observations."

Well, scientists posit (eternally unprovable) the whole idea(*-Theory!) of an objective universe to frame their observations and resultant sub-theories, and sometimes posit things which are later proven false. ;)

"There is no one central "if A = B and B = C then A = C" that we all tap into."

I realize you think that. Question: why? Do you evidence? Would you say there are no electrons? No other minds? Electrons and minds explain your inner-experiences. So does universal logic."

My evidence is prima facia, me thinking, in my proximal mind with my created concepts and me applying the discipline that I should not contradict myself. I first grasped/conceived the semantics of that logical truth by constructing the idea from interpreting the symbols in a school text. Again, as paper and ink there is no proposition as such. I created my personal copy of this truth by applying the correct meanings to the symbols I saw. No direct contact with other minds, and no access to anything like a 'central source' of living concepts. On the other hand, it would seem that any alternative theory would/could not have any evidence. As long as 'universal logic' intends to mean the independent ability (varying) of every mind to achieve self-consistency, then fine, but irrelevant to my personal ability

198

and accomplishments of coherency. I believe there is an objective universe, and that there are electrons, based on my reading, exposure to other media etc. Some other people don't. But *if* the objective universe exists, there is zero evidence or even logically coherent definitions that would place anything named 'logic' out there, let alone that it would be directly accessible to your mind. All you have are your constructs and your desire to be self-consistent. Electrons may 'explain' a brain, but not a mind, they are logically utterly separate. Tell your honorable wife that you love her "because electrons" and you will get the same generous condescension as when you tried modal 'logic' to discuss whether you scratched the car. :)

"Well, I already demonstrated that transcendent logic is needed at the start of this thread."

Where please? requote it. You have said (if I understand it) that 'transcendent logic' could explain why we agree that "A=A" is a good hygiene to maintain in a logically coherent structure. I'd say it is because we communicated, and because we each wanted to be self-consistent, and we found that our individual copies of "A=A" are semantically identical. Nothing transcendent logic-wise. We could say we seemingly successfully transcend our factual subjective isolation in/to our own mind, by mutually bearing that chain of faith-based presumptions that lead to our symbol-based communications.

"The subsequent emails were about clarifying terms so you could understand the proof I provided. But here you say that nothing else

is even possible. Maybe it would serve your system to provide a proof of the impossibility."

If we define the mind as the subjective space-time, and defining as I did, subjective and objective so they are mathematically, utterly disjoint, that would be the basis. 'Transcendent' would then have to be defined, but would likely be defused as some partition within ones' mind, because nothing crosses the objective/subjective divide. Subjectively, all you have is the mental flow of your personal private experiential input, and thence your personal interpretation/modelling of it. You *only* experience *your* experiences, with/in *your* mind. The only transcendence is a via a chain, based on 1) the assumption/faith that there *is* anything else, ie: the objective universe, (or any other externality) somehow (from a rigidly logical, proximal experiential/subjective perspective) is a leap of faith, then to presume that any of those seeming objects in your visual field (which you think represents the objective universe) are moving and making sounds which make it easy/plausible for you to imagine/induce them as sentient and self-motivating like you, etc.

"That will help you make clear the underlying premises of your system. We both agree that logic depends on a mind. But how do you deduce that all the logic you access depends on your mind? If you could deduce that, you could become famous! I'm serious."

Cool. It seems simple, based on the utter impossibility of *deducing* anything other than my mind. *Inducing*, on statistical evidences, and in choosing aesthetically between equally unprovable options, sure, just like we induce the existence of electrons. But *deduce*? I think my position irreplaceably holds the deductive logical high ground.

Josh:

"Good, and we only ever have direct, deducible access to our own."

Why do you think that?

Or are you saying that you cannot see how to access a mind that is external to your own? Do you think I exist? How?"

"I declare, almost by definition, that we only have direct deducible, actually axiomatic experience, necessarily private in/of our own mind, per the elementary clarity of Solipsism' challenge! We each only experience *our* sole and private experiences, a stream of temporal transactions with us as the focus of particular stimuli. No one can ever logically prove that any of these stimuli are anything but the mind's self-generated imaginations, as opposed to a (preferable and tempting) faithful representation of some truly extant and separate externality. It is only our personal, varying, and eminently fallible efforts of interpretation that would posit any externality *behind* the stimulus. I say 'behind' because even if you posit that your axiomatic pain represents a forgotten Lego piece on the bathroom floor, it is your internal representation of that Lego piece, and the floor and a foot) that you are interacting with in your mind. The actual Lego piece is separate, out there (or not) a non-experiential thing. You may proceed on your assumption, and then even find that your conceptualization was completely wrong, that the object was totally different, or even not there, if you somehow suffered a quick onset of plantar fasciitis. Indeed some people who have factually lost a limb still have serious 'phantom pain' from it.

In my real life, I have no practical doubt that the objective realm exists, and that you exist like I do, in a body imagining things in your mind, and that we've successfully co-opted some little bits of the mindless objective world between us to generate, send, receive and interpret symbols to convey meaning to one another."

Good! That's what I thought. :)

"Scientists posit electrons to explain their observations. Similarly, you can posit a mind (and logic) outside of your own mind to explain your observations.

Well, scientists posit the whole idea of an objective universe to frame their observations and resultant theories, and posit things which are later proven false. ;)"

;)

"There is no one central "if A = B and B = C then A = C" that we all tap into."

Why do you think that?

I realize you think that. Question: why? Do you evidence? Would you say there are no electrons? No other minds? Electrons and minds explain your inner-experiences. So does universal logic."

"My evidence is prima facia, me thinking, in my proximal mind with my created concepts and me applying the discipline that I should not contradict myself. On the other hand, it would seem that any alternative theory would/could not have any evidence. *My* credulity that my model of reality, which includes my concepts of electrons and other minds, which I project to exist, seems largely unchallenged statistically by my ongoing experiences, but that is not logical proof I am right. 'Universal logic' doesn't either. All that is necessary or evident is *my* logic."

Why would it seem that way?

"I believe there is an objective universe, and that there are electrons. Some other people don't. But *if* the objective universe exists, there is zero evidence or even logically coherent definitions that would place anything named 'logic' out there, let alone that it would be directly accessible to your mind."

Well, I gave a proof, and while you may not have been persuaded by it, I still see nothing wrong with it. Every step is as clear in my mind as the laws of logic themselves. ;)

"All you have are your constructs and your desire to be self-consistent. Electrons may 'explain' a brain, but not a mind, they are logically utterly separate. Tell your honorable wife that you love her "because electrons" and you will get the same generous condescension as when you tried modal logic' to discuss whether you scratched the car. :)"

Nice!

"Well, I already demonstrated that transcendent logic is needed at the start of this thread."

Where please? requote it."

I have a rule against repeating. You are welcome to revisit anything in this thread, including your responses and my follow-up clarifications.

You have said (if I understand it) that 'transcendent logic' could explain why we agree that "A=A" is a good hygiene to maintain in a logically coherent structure. I'd say it is because we communicated, and because we each wanted to be self-consistent.

So just to clarify, I gave two types of arguments. One was a proof. That was the first email in this thread. Later, just to provide an abundance of riches, I also gave an argument from predictive success. Your response is the right strategy -- in principle -- which is to provide an alternative account of the data in question. But note: merely providing an alternative account is insufficient to show that it is a better account (in terms of simplicity, predictive power, intrinsic probability, etc).

"The subsequent emails were about clarifying terms so you could understand the proof I provided. But here you say that nothing else *is even possible. Maybe it would serve your system to provide a proof of the impossibility."*

"If we define the mind as the subjective space-time, and defining as I did, subjective and objective so they are mathematically, utterly disjoint, that would be the basis. 'Transcendent' would then have to be defined, but would likely be defused as some partition within ones' mind, because nothing crosses the objective/subjective divide. Subjectively, all you have is the mental flow of your personal private experiential input, and thence your personal interpretation/modelling of it. You *only* experience *your* experiences, with/in *your* mind."

True, but why think you can't also experience elements of another mind within your own mind. If logic were an element of a universal mind, why think you couldn't experience this element from within your own mind. Even if all were purely subjective, why think different subjects couldn't access any elements of each other? Do you have a proof of that? Can you develop it in terms of axioms and theorems?

"The only transcendence is a via a chain, based on 1) the assumption/faith that there *is* anything else, ie: the objective universe, somehow (from a rigidly logical, proximal experiential/subjective perspective) is a leap of faith, then to presume that any of those seeming objects in your visual field are moving and making sounds which make it easy/plausible for you to imagine/induce them as sentient and self-motivating like you, etc."

"That will help you make clear the underlying premises of your system. We both agree that logic depends on a mind. But how do you deduce that all the logic you access depends on your mind? If you could deduce that, you could become famous! I'm serious."

"Cool. It seems simple, based on the utter impossibility of *deducing* anything other than my mind."

'Why think that's impossible? Where's the deduction of impossibility?'

"*Inducing*, on statistical evidences, and in choosing aesthetically between equally unprovable options, sure, just like we induce the existence of electrons. But *deduce*? I think my position irreplaceably holds the deductive logical high ground."

Nice phrase. :)

I like you.

Best,

Josh

Joe:

""Good, and we only ever have direct, deducible access to our own.

"Why do you think that?"

Because we are at the core, purely experiential, and all occurs to us, in our mind, and that anything, any concept we have that we decide is to represent something beyond our mind is inductive speculation, still an act within our mind. The basic challenge of Solipsism is that you will never have logical deductive proof that *anything* exists besides/beyond your mind and imaginations. There is a walk-in burger stand near UC Berkeley with a sign posted "NO TALKING TO INVISIBLE PEOPLE". Even just invoking the OCCAM heuristic, it is simpler to posit that your thoughts are your own, your visions are your own, and that the invisible people that some denizens were talking to, were similarly figments of their own construction. By 'direct', I distinguish it from the objective-world-and-internet-accessible indirect accesses/inferences.

I never access your mind, and you never access mine. We know of each other and our respective contents only by interpreting symbols passed along that long chain. You may desire to posit some other sort of 'special mind' that is not your own, that magically protrudes into yours, but there will and can be no evidence to you, that can provably distinguish that metaphor from your simply making/thinking everything up, and just not believing you are the author of some of it.

"There is no one central "if A = B and B = C then A = C" that we all tap into.

"Why do you think that?"

As above. There is no heft or meaning to "A=A" in my mind, the only place where anything really matters to me, except as I deem and understand it, and in order to understand it I must construct it myself. The same for you. Ideas are not latent anywhere, just like all the infinite numbers that represent points on a line are not 'fully instantiated and waiting latent to be cited", they are only constructed/expressed individually as needed, created algorithmically by formula.

"My evidence is prima facia, me thinking, in my proximal mind with my created concepts and me applying the discipline that I should not contradict myself. On the other hand, it would seem that any alternative theory would/could not have any evidence.

"Why would it seem that way?"

Well, 'seeming' is a personal private experience, involving only me and the images/ideas being 'seemed'. To add anyone or anything else in the picture/experience is unwarranted/unnecessary for the seeming to happen. Me and my thoughts. I want them to play well together, I want an integrated body of truth. If two ideas conflict, I am going to take the position that one or both are false, and I will try to fix it, and not rely on either as much until I do. Logic is only defineable within a given mind. I can believe "A" and you can believe "not A", and logic is not involved. But I cannot believe 'A' and 'not A' if I want to adhere to logic, self-consistency. And some do believe both, or neither, and live long happy lives without concern for logic.

"Well, I gave a proof, and while you may not have been persuaded by it, I still see nothing wrong with it. Every step is as clear in my mind as the laws of logic themselves. ;)"

"I have a rule against repeating. You are welcome to revisit anything in this thread, including your responses and my follow-up clarifications."

OK, fair enough, let me look. I would hold 'proof' as 'logically unquestionable"...

"So just to clarify, I gave two types of arguments. One was a proof. That was the first email in this thread. Later, just to provide an abundance of riches, I also gave an argument from predictive success. Your response is the right strategy -- in principle -- which is to provide an alternative account of the data in question. But note: merely providing an alternative account is insufficient to show that it is a better account (in terms of simplicity, predictive power, intrinsic probability, etc)."

Sure. simplicity, predictive power, 'intrinsic probability' etc are among the tests/heuristics to be specifically applied to competing theories. And when such theories are about anything other than the proximal contents of your own mind, such as mathematics, but rather are about something independent of the testers' mind, then tests and heuristics can only falsify, not prove, just like physics.

"If we define the mind as the subjective space-time, and defining as I did, subjective and objective so they are mathematically,

utterly disjoint, that would be the basis. 'Transcendent' would then have to be defined, but would likely be defused as some partition within ones' mind, because nothing crosses the objective/subjective divide. Subjectively, all you have is the mental flow of your personal private experiential input, and thence your personal interpretation/modelling of it. You *only* experience *your* experiences, with/in *your* mind."

"True, but why think you can't also experience elements of another mind within your own mind."

Privacy policy, declared sovereignty (;) * 0.5) It's all mine. Practically, when considering any other mind I believe of, and necessarily likening such minds to my own, the only mind I really know, I never drop anything into someone else's mind, mind-to-mind, nor do I ever stumble on something that I suspect my mother left there, except as was recovered from where it was first actually installed, at a previous time from the standard prosaic transcendences such as nagging by phone or email etc. So the 'other mind that I'd access from within my mind would most likely be a model of a mind, I made and populated with ideas, or designated a categorization by which I would determine whether any given new idea I had came from my open/admitted personal construction, or whether I would deem it 'as from this other mind'. You could do that, but you'd never be able to prove a functional distinction between that partitioning as a model of this other real-and-odd sidecar mind, and you making it all up.

"If logic were an element of a universal mind, why think you couldn't experience this element from within your own mind. Even if all were purely subjective, why think different subjects couldn't access any elements of each other? Do you have a proof of that? Can you develop it in terms of axioms and theorems?"

Logic is not 'an element'. It is an observable/testable relationship between related ideas/assertions. Logic is 'demonstrated in other minds' only by your imagining the ideas you believe are in that other mind (obtained only by internet ;)) and your checking the string of assertions for inconsistency as you understand and enforce it in your own back yard. Logic is a temporal achievement of active thought. As to axioms, your mind is axiomatic. Any other mind is at best a theorem, and the less it is like your own mind, the less likely the theorem is to be true.

"I like you."

I *really* like you too, and am greatly heartened to be liked for this my most deep and socially centrifugal realm of thought.

Much thanks.

Josh:

""Good, and we only ever have direct, deducible access to our own.

Why do you think that?"

Because we are at the core, purely experiential, and all occurs to us, in our mind, and that anything, any concept we have that we decide is to represent something beyond our mind is inductive speculation, still an act within our mind. The basic challenge of Solipsism is that you will never have logical deductive proof that *anything* exists besides/beyond your mind and imaginations. There is a walk-in burger stand near UC Berkeley with a sign posted "NO TALKING TO INVISIBLE PEOPLE". Even just invoking the OCCAM heuristic, it is simpler to posit that your thoughts are your own, your visions are your own, and that the invisible people that some denizens were talking to, were similarly figments of their own construction. By 'direct', I distinguish it from the objective-world-and-internet-accessible indirect accesses/inferences."

Good, add it to the book!

"I never access your mind, and you never access mine. We know of each other and our respective contents only by interpreting symbols passed along that long chain."

"To be honest, I think that's true for contingent minds. But I think that a necessary, universal mind could be touched directly within each mind.

You may desire to posit some other sort of 'special mind' that is not your own, that magically protrudes into yours, but there will and can be no evidence to you, that can provably distinguish that metaphor from your simply making/thinking everything up, and just not believing you are the author of some of it."

Except, I gave a proof. ;)

"There is no one central "if A = B and B = C then A = C" that we all tap into.

"Why do you think that?"

As above. There is no heft or meaning to "A=A" in my mind, the only place where anything really matters to me, except as I deem and understand it, and in order to understand it I must construct it myself. The same for you. Ideas are not latent anywhere, just like all the infinite numbers that represent points on a line are not 'fully instantiated and waiting latent to be cited", they are only constructed/expressed individually as needed, created algorithmically by formula."

More good metaphors / imagery. Add to your book. :)

"My evidence is prima facia, me thinking, in my proximal mind with my created concepts and me applying the discipline that I should not contradict myself. On the other hand, it would seem that any alternative theory would/could not have any evidence.

"Why would it seem that way?"

Well, 'seeming' is a personal private experience, involving only me and the images/ideas being 'seemed'.

"I just want to emphasize here the difference between the experience of seeing and the thing seen. Seeing is within, but it doesn't follow that what you see directly exists only within, or that there is no way to see that it also exists out of sight. My hope, to be frank, is that as you spell out the premises in your own argument you will see clearly this distinction and critical inference in your system."

To add anyone or anything else in the picture/experience is unwarranted/unnecessary for the seeming to happen. Me and my thoughts. I want them to play well together, I want an integrated body of truth. If two ideas conflict, I am going to take the position that one or both are false, and I will try to fix it, and not rely on either as much until I do.

Nice!

Logic is only defineable within a given mind. I can believe "A" and you can believe "not A", and logic is not involved. But I cannot believe 'A' and 'not A' if I want to adhere to logic, self-consistency. And some do believe both, or neither, and live long happy lives without concern for logic.

"Well, I gave a proof, and while you may not have been persuaded by it, I still see nothing wrong with it. Every step is as clear in my mind as the laws of logic themselves. ;)"

"I have a rule against repeating. You are welcome to revisit anything in this thread, including your responses and my follow-up clarifications."

OK, fair enough, let me look. I would hold 'proof' as 'logically unquestionable'...

"So just to clarify, I gave two types of arguments. One was a proof. That was the first email in this thread. Later, just to provide an abundance of riches, I also gave an argument from predictive success. Your response is the right strategy -- in principle -- which is to provide an alternative account of the data in question. But note: merely providing an alternative account is insufficient to show that it is a better account (in terms of simplicity, predictive power, intrinsic probability, etc)."

Sure. simplicity, predictive power, 'intrinsic probability' etc are among the tests/heuristics to be specifically applied to competing theories. And when such theories are about anything other than the proximal contents of your own mind, such as mathematics, but rather are about something independent of the testers' mind, then tests and heuristics can only falsify, not prove, just like physics.

"If we define the mind as the subjective space-time, and defining as I did, subjective and objective so they are mathematically, utterly disjoint, that would be the basis. 'Transcendent' would then have to be defined, but would likely be defused as some partition within ones' mind, because nothing crosses the objective/subjective divide. Subjectively, all you have is the mental flow of your personal private experiential input, and thence your personal interpretation/modelling of it. You *only* experience *your* experiences, with/in *your* mind."

"True, but why think you can't also experience elements of another mind within your own mind."

"Privacy policy, declared sovereignty (;) * 0.5) It's all mine."

:)

"Practically, when considering any other mind I believe of, and necessarily likening such minds to my own, the only mind I really know, I never drop anything into someone elses' mind, mind-to-mind, nor do I ever stumble on something that I suspect my mother left there, except as was recovered from where it was first actually installed, at a previous time from the standard prosaic transcendences such as nagging by phone or email etc. So the 'other mind that I'd access from within my mind would most likely"

"most likely? Are you showing something to be impossible or improbable?"

"be a model of a mind, I made and populated with ideas, or designated a categorization by which I would determine whether any given new idea I had came from my open/admitted personal construction, or whether I would deem it 'as from this other mind'. You could do that, but you'd never be able to prove a functional distinction between that partitioning as a model of this other real-and-odd sidecar mind, and you making it all up."

That's the assumption I question. I say the light of logic itself points to its own distinction from your thoughts of that same light. You say otherwise. I want proof! :) I challenge you only to sharpen your system and project.

"If logic were an element of a universal mind, why think you couldn't experience this element from within your own mind. Even if all were purely subjective, why think different subjects couldn't access any elements of each other? Do you have a proof of that? Can you develop it in terms of axioms and theorems?

Logic is not 'an element'. It is an observable/testable relationship between related ideas/assertions *in a given mind*."

That's fine. I meant "element" in a broad sense to cover anything.

"Logic is 'demonstrated in other minds' only by your imagining the ideas you believe are in that other mind (obtained only by internet ;)) and your checking the string of assertions for inconsistency as you understand and enforce it in your own back yard. Logic is a temporal achievement of active thought. As to axioms, your mind is axiomatic. Any other mind is at best a theorem, and the less it is like your own mind, the less likely the theorem is to be true."

"I like you."

"I *really* like you too, and am greatly heartened to be liked for this my most deep and socially centrifugal realm of thought.

Much thanks."

You are welcome, my friend!

Joe:

""I never access your mind, and you never access mine. We know of each other and our respective contents only by interpreting symbols passed along that long chain.

To be honest, I think that's true for contingent minds. But I think that a necessary, universal mind could be touched directly within each mind."

The term 'contingent mind' is inapt in my ontology. Subjectively, as/how you live, there is one a-priori mind, non-contingent mind, necessary mind, on which *everything* else depends. *Yours. *Nothing* else is necessary. There are attributes, capabilities, facilities of our mind, subjectively just there, a-priori, unexplained, and sometimes not even specifically recognized, or even (I propose) misattributed to outside origin. The chief two arenas of the mind, which are brilliantly plumbed, described and tested in Kahneman's "Thinking, Fast and Slow', are the fully conscious articulating part where we can verbally calculate and reason, and the powerful subconscious 'reaction engine' which operates continually, semi-autonomously, interpreting real-time stimuli and instantly presenting the conscious mind with rich and plausible representations, crucially including immediate and palpable aesthetic/survival value judgments, such that there need be no explicit thought, and that an immediate self-interested physical response is practically ready-mapped to take. It is this latter, fast-and-always-on intuition engine that can also take on consciously posed questions/problems, questions or conundrums one may pose to oneself. I believe this 'intuition engine' is not like a typical computer, but well may be like a 'quantum computer' where all possibilities are organically mulled at once, and that eventually a plausible resolution comes into focus as the haze of side-connections disburses. This is then revealed with an aesthetically detectable sense of relief, sometimes long after the problem was self-posed by the thinker. I believe that some people do not credit themselves with this capability, nor perhaps will some of them be attracted by the independence, isolation, subjectivity, and responsibility this personal capability would imply, and that they would rather see it as a portal to a more reliable 'objective' externality, like a special 'other mind' that reads your mind, and then later 'reveals' answers, not as a normal mind-to-mind communication, based on parsed language, but as a plausible story/image replete and redolent with final judgments and feelings.

'Universal' is most rigorously logically defined as the full reach and imagination of your mind. How/whether you parse your experience as in part implying anything beyond your mind, is speculation, unnecessary for your existence and operation at the center of your subjective space-time.

You may desire to posit some other sort of 'special mind' that is not your own, that magically protrudes into yours, but there will and can be no evidence to you, that can provably distinguish that metaphor from your simply making/thinking everything up, and just not believing you are the author of some of it.

"Except, I gave a proof. ;)"

Which I already rejected as a proof, with reasons, and an alternative, which even if it only drops the probability of your hypothesis being true to a 'fair and balanced 50%' , it can no longer be called a proof.

"I just want to emphasize here the difference between the experience of seeing and the thing seen. Seeing is within, but it doesn't follow that what you see directly exists only within, or that there is no way to see that it also exists out of sight. My hope, to be frank, is that as you spell out the premises in your own argument you will see clearly this distinction and critical inference in your system."

Yes. The experience of seeing requires the seer and the specific thing seen in the field of vision. If the thing seen is explicitly only an internal construct, such as we agree pure mathematics is, then we can say the '2's, the '+', the '=', and the '4' only exist within, as/when considered/remembered. Even if we posit a 'we' and that others do math, we can imagine them with their own '2's etc, which function the same, but are still different instances. On the other hand, if we 'see' an apple, we are in fact interpreting a matrix of nerve actions/inactions that we can posit is a processed model of bio-bits we interpret as an image *representing* something outside us, whose reflected light was previously inverted by our cornea and converted to bio-electric signals. We do tend to project that image to represent (or naively/practically *be*) an objective distal object, non-experiential in/of itself, but a passive party to our experience, based on its reflectivity of light when we looked at it. We will never have pure deductive logic, from our subjective position to verify there's an apple out there, let alone when we ponder an object that we simply remember, or hypothesize to exist out there. There is no doubt of your *internal* 'seeing' of the unicorn, or 'a good five-cent cigar' in your mind, but logical chastity regarding the external, non-experiential things we imagine/interpret requires doubt and will only bear relativistic statistical inductive evidences/arguments for their actual existence.

"Practically, when considering any other mind I believe of, and necessarily likening such minds to my own, the only mind I really know, I never drop anything into someone elses' mind, mind-to-mind, nor do I ever stumble on something that I suspect my mother left there, except as was recovered from where it was first actually installed, at a previous time from the standard prosaic transcendences such as nagging by phone or email etc. So the 'other mind that I'd access from within my mind would most likely *most likely? Are you showing something to be impossible or improbable?"*

"Inductively less reasonable. We cannot prove to the wino that the pink elephant is not there, and that they are imagining it rather than that we are blind or conspiring gas-lighters… But I present an alternative to the 'other mind' metaphor, which generates the same functionality (if not, for some, the same aesthetics or foundational comfort) from the individual mind itself.

"be a model of a mind, I made and populated with ideas, or designated a categorization by which I would determine whether any given new idea I had came from my open/admitted personal construction, or whether I would deem it 'as from this other mind'. You could do that, but you'd never be able to prove a functional distinction between that partitioning as a model of this other real-and-odd sidecar mind, and you making it all up.

That's the assumption I question. I say the light of logic itself points to its own distinction from your thoughts of that same light. You say otherwise. I want proof! :) I challenge you only to sharpen your system and project."

Always! The 'light of logic' needs to be defined, but to stay rigorous, logic is an attribute of coherency in a chain of thoughts. As such, it is plainly not the left-side 'A', nor the '=', nor the right-side 'A', nor the even the full equation, but if I then say 'if A = B and B = C, then A = C', the logic is in the consideration of the enforced coherence. This is the clear distinction as I've shown in examples previously, where if there is only one person awake, and all he's doing is thinking 'I like pie" there is no logic to be seen anywhere. Logic is demonstrated by someone's success/consistency in correlated thoughts. I can't see another way to exemplify logic, let alone that it would somehow lead mandatorily outside my mind. Again, I may be the solitary largely unself-aware God, imagining *all*. That's the simplest tack..."

Josh:

"Which I already rejected as a proof, with reasons, and an alternative

Well, you rejected the proof you interpreted in your mind, but not the one in my mind. ;)

In any case, at some point in your book, it may help you reach your goals to develop a strict deduction in first-order predicate logic. For example, see if can translate your last paragraph from your previous email into formal logic. I'm not saying this because I think you can't do it. I'm saying it because I think you could do it, and doing it would help make very precise how your system is built.

Best,

Josh

Joe:

"OK, so tell me how what I saw as your proof, based on what you typed, is different than what is on your mind. :)"

Here is how I disproved what you typed:

"The next thing to see is that The Law of Identity is distinct from my individual thoughts about identity. That's because my individual thoughts are distinct from each other. To see this inference clearly, consider my thought this morning about identity. That thought is is not the same thought as my more recent thought about identity. The thoughts are similar (maybe even exactly similar), but they are not one and the same thought. Yet, if these individual thoughts were the The Law of Identity, then they would be one and the same thought. But they aren't the same thought. So they are not The Law of Identity. Q.E.D."

I am not sure what is being asserted then proven, but yes, the two thoughts are identical in function, but distinct temporally, even if only in the one necessary mind, yours. Yes, the thought "A=A" is not the thought 'The Law Of Identity'. "The Law Of Identity" is a separate thought, a concept, a label, a qualification, a generalization you can assign to, or assert about any instance of "A=A", or "B=B" etc. (But it is just an assertion, and while it can exist in your mind independent of any other assertion, even examples of it, it does not, nor need not exist when you are not thinking/asserting it. No transcendence needed or possible. It's in/of your head when/as it exists, no different than 'I like pie'.)

"So far we have established from my starting definitions that the Law of Identity is distinct from my individual thoughts about identity. In other words, the Law of Identity transcends my individual thoughts about identity."

No. It does not transcend. It simply exists separately and independently. A person can know and employ the self-assurance/discipline that "A=A", even implicitly by holding such analogously true for every symbol they use in an algebraic proof, one that might not use the symbol 'A' at all, without explicitly stating/holding that "A=A", though he/she would have to if they were in an axiomatic math class. Absent that irritating class, there is no need for, no transcendence of, the generality or the label when using/thinking/assuming "A=A", and symmetrically there is no transcendence or need for "A=A" when pondering The Law Of Identity.

And yes, I will consider doing some formal logical expressions/translations. I do try to make extreme clarity with English and definitions, but I infer from 'the industry' that there is a valuable audience that would be swayed/enticed if some of my crucial, and perfectly defined expressions were translated from English to formal logic, something I studied 30 years ago... If I find a philosopher as smart as you, with time on their hands, who grasps what we have been saying, maybe I could hire them to collaborate on the translation. I would seem so much smarter if I included that... (:) * 0.5)"

Josh:

"We've now moved, and I am now ready to address your previous note.

<<

OK, so tell me how what I saw as your proof, based on what you typed, is different than what is on your mind. :)

Here is how I disproved what you typed:

"The next thing to see is that The Law of Identity is distinct from my individual thoughts about identity. That's because my individual thoughts are distinct from each other. To see this inference clearly, consider my thought this morning about identity. That thought is is not the same thought as my more recent thought about identity. The thoughts are similar (maybe even exactly similar), but they are not one and the same thought. Yet, if these individual thoughts were the The Law of Identity, then they would be one and the same thought. But they aren't the same thought. So they are not The Law of Identity. Q.E.D."

"I am not sure what is being asserted then proven, but yes, the two thoughts are identical in function, but distinct temporally, even if only in the one necessary mind, yours. Yes, the thought "A=A" is not the thought 'The Law Of Identity'. "The Law Of Identity" is a separate thought, a concept, a label, a qualification, a generalization you can assign to, or assert about any instance of "A=A", or "B=B" etc. (But it is just an assertion, and while it can exist in your mind independent of any other assertion, even examples of it, it does not, nor need not exist when you are not thinking/asserting it. No transcendence needed or possible. It's in/of your head when/as it exists, no different than 'I like pie.')"

Maybe it would help to label the steps in my argument so we can see which step, if any, you are addressing.

Start with Definitions.

D1. Let 'L' abbreviate "that A=A, for all A" (The Law of Identity).

D2. Let T1 = your thought that L at time t1.

D3. Let T2 = your thought that L at some different time t2.

Now for my proposed proof:

1. T1 ≠ T2. (By Leibniz's law of identity, since they occur at different times)

2. If the Law of Identity is the same as your thought that L, then T1 = the Law of Identity and T2 = the Law of Identity (by definitions D1 & D2).

3. But the consequent in (2) contradicts (1).

4. Therefore, the Law of Identity is not the same as your thought that L. (By contraposition)

To be clear, this conclusion does not say that the Law of Identity is not itself a thought. Rather, it says that it is not merely your thought.

Another, independent avenue to the same result is from invariance. I know we've talked about this before, but I take it as obvious that the laws of logic hold true constantly, whereas you do not hold any of your thoughts constantly.

So that's how things look to me, anyway. :)

Hope you've been well, my friend.

Joe:

Yes, T1 is not the same object as T2, nor would it be if you and I each thought the same thing at the same time. They might be identical in function as we would each use our copy, but by virtue of existing (only) at different times or places, they are unique. In fact, each A in the assertion 'A=A' is a different instance, even as we are declaring that they will be identical in function/meaning.

The mistake is to declare/think that there is just one law of identity while we agree that T1 is not the same thing as T2. To be exact, there is no *one* Law Of Identity. T1 is my LOI at time 1, T2 is your LOI at time 2, T3 is my LOI when I recall it again, the next day. Each of them are functionally identical in their respective contexts. All instances of LOI are functionally, semantically identical, mind-invariant, but each/every instance is absolutely dependent on, and functional only in the mind that is currently positing if. The term 'Law' is nothing more than any other assertion, any other thought, with no privilege or place or existence or need, beyond whenever it or any other assertion is asserted, and is always unique and private to the current asserter. Assertions and Laws are just thoughts. There is certainly a scale and spectrum of reliability/provability of assertions, of which laws are a perhaps more personally trusted subset, and for which high axioms are logically a most-trusted, even undeniable subset of laws, etc, but they are *all* *just* *thoughts*. No evidence of, utility of, possibility of, or meaning of any thought as such except as the thought/assertion/law/axiom is actively (and always privately) being thought.

So, the law, any law, any assertion true or false is unique-and-limited to the mind+time it is being pondered/posited. The next instant when the topic is lunch, any previous T/assertion vanishes harmlessly as such. Analogous, functionally identical-but-also-unique-according the key of mind+time, are freely produced/thought when desired/useful again.

And thanks for your care. I must say my cancer has metastasized to places that can cause sharp periodic pain, between times (for now) which are still rewarding and fun. But the ability of current medicine to treat pancreatic cancer as it progresses is getting thinner and more compromising. I will now be doing chemo every week, and there is no promise that it will halt, let alone cure... I am foreseeing a physician-assisted graceful exit at some point unless there is a miracle. Wish me luck

But note well that yours and my conversation is a local peak of the good times.

Love and unparalleled respect,

Joe

Josh:

"Yes, T1 is not the same object as T2, nor would it be if you and I each thought the same thing at the same time. They might be identical in function as we would each use our copy, but by virtue of existing (only) at different times or places, they are unique. In fact, each A in the assertion 'A=A' is a different instance, even as we are declaring that they will be identical in function/meaning."

Right.

"The mistake is to declare/think that there is just one law of identity while we agree that T1 is not the same thing as T2. The term 'Law' is nothing more than any other assertion, any other thought, with no privilege or place or existence or need, beyond whenever it or any other assertion is asserted, and is always unique and private to the current asserter. Assertions and Laws are just thoughts. There is certainly a scale and spectrum of reliability/provability of assertions, of which laws are a per-haps more personally trusted subset, and for which high axioms are logically a most-trusted, even undeniable subset of laws, etc, but they are *all* *just* *thoughts*. No evidence of, utility of, possibility of, or meaning of any thought as such except as the thought/assertion/law/axiom is actively (and always privately) being thought."

Good points. Maybe I can clarify one thought that I didn't express so well before. Even if there are many Laws Of Identity (one per thought that L), these different laws have something in common. As you said, they might be identical in function. Great! So call this something - this function - Q. When I was using the term "Law of Identity," I was referring to Q. Not sure if that helps clarifies anything.

"So, the law, any law, any assertion true or false is unique-and-limited to the mind+time it is being pondered/posited. The next instant when the topic is lunch, any previous T/assertion vanishes harmlessly as such. Analogous, functionally identical-but-also-unique-according the key of mind+time, are freely produced/thought when desired/useful again.

And thanks for your care. I must say my cancer has metastasized to places that can cause sharp periodic pain, between times (for now) which are still rewarding and fun. But the ability of current medicine to treat pancreatic cancer as it progresses is getting thinner and more compromising. I will now be doing chemo every week, and there is no promise that it will halt, let alone cure... I am foreseeing a physician-assisted graceful exit at some point unless there is a miracle. Wish me luck"

Awwww, that sounds rough. I really want you to get better. Your work and existence are of great value.

Joe:

"Good points. Maybe I can clarify one thought that I didn't express so well before. Even if there are many Laws Of Identity (one per thought that L), these different laws have something in common. As you said, they might be identical in function. Great! So call this something - this function - Q. When I was using the term "Law of Identity," I was referring to Q. Not sure if that helps clarifies anything."

Yes, they are identical, but that is just to say that they can be classified as members of a set one defines as "The law of identity". They are not connected themselves, and one could exist fully without the other. Just like a marble in Ruanda is (for the sake of argument) identical to a marble that was in Fort Worth 100 years ago, they are still utterly independent. *They* share nothing. It is only the observer that links them in his/her mind, by their criteria if/when he/she does. Are they the same because of geometric shape? Does size matter? Mineral content, yeah or nay? Need they both be 'cats eyes'? Commonality, like beauty, is in the eye of the beholder/classifier.

The only important commonality between two instances of L, are that they were created, individually and separately as needed, for the purpose of the mind that needed/wanted it at the time, like shoes the Etruscans made have something in common with Nikes today. Nothing though, outside the minds' intents. The commonality is because of the similarity of minds, not that there is somehow only one mind. There is *nothing*, again, extant, defineable, let alone fungible about any idea/assertion/law other than as generated just-in-time as a live thought by an active thinker. If her or another thinker creates identical thoughts it is only because they independently have identical purposes. Nothing else needed, nothing else possible... Nothing thought or feeling-related extant except in an individual mind at the time.

There may be two objects with practically nothing in common except they were both used, at different times and places, as a paperweight or weapon. The 'Q' resides only in the mind.

Josh:

"The 'Q' resides only in the mind."

Sweet agreement.

And that takes us back to the question of what "the mind" refers to. Maybe we are going around in a large circle, where every trip hopefully contributes to clarity, if nothing else. :)

"*They* share nothing."

Here may be the crux. My understanding of "x is similar to y" is that "x share something in common with y." I take it that instances of L are similar in some respect. So it seems to me, from my understanding of "similarity," that they share something (call it a "set" or whatever).

But maybe we also agree here. For I agree that they share nothing apart from a mind. After all, on my understanding, logic is perfect thinking, and the home of perfect thinking is a perfect mind -- one who, by its perfection, loves you from within you. Or so it seems to me from my limited perspective. :)

Best,

Josh

Joe:

"The 'Q' is you. X and Y do not intrinsically 'share' anything. They just *are*, separately and unconcernedly. It is *you that anoints them with similarity according to your taste and perspective. *You* define the set, the criteria for generalization. You gather them up conceptually, as/when desired and they do not change when/whether you gather them in your mind or when/whether you stop associating them at all.

Perfect thinking is an optional but a tiny bit florid alternative to 'coherent thinking', but it can exist in any mind, along with cases of imperfect/incoherent thinking, flashes of clear light, along with sputtering sparks like failed bulbs, and objectively times of no activity at all. If/whenever you get '2+2=4', you win. Perfect.

There is no need, purpose or effect of these thoughts other than for the private interests of the mind like yours.

You love yourself, necessarily. Nothing external needed or possible. Love is 'identification with', 'attachment to', etc, and the one axiomatic 'identification' is you 'with your self', that which you cannot escape, you yourself. You can approach whatever 'perfection' you like, as testable by the coherence of your assembled thoughts. This coherence give one confidence in themselves. And there can be no confidence in anything else except to the degree you are self-confident.

There is nothing sure, apart from *your* mind, even if you only ignore the centricity of yourself, and only imagine something other. No thought is necessary, and only one mind is necessary, yours.

Josh:

"X and Y do not intrinsically 'share' anything."

We've isolated the point at issue. For my part, I do not understand what "x is similar to y" means if they do not share something in common. That's how it looks to me, anyway, from my own limited perspective.

That said, your emphasis on the primacy of one's self and perspective is also something I resonate with and find helpful and valuable.

Best,

Josh

Joe:

OK! Yes, X and Y do not share anything intrinsically. They are *similar TO YOU*. Two grains of sand, which by happenstance (or even intent!) have the exact same makeup and dimensions, nevertheless have a different history, totally different population of atoms, necessarily separate geometrical location, etc. They need not interact nor affect each other in any way. In fact one of them may have existed as such, before the other, and its prior state is/was in no way affected by the subsequent creation of the second one. They may not both even exist as such at any intersection of time. Again, they (or any X and Y) do not share anything intrinsically. It is *you* who creates the logical set in which you anoint them (your internal representation of them) as members. They 'share' nothing except in your mind, as/when you claim them as related according to your tastes and specs, and this association you make in your mind also has no effect on them intrinsically, whether/when you do or don't 'give them something to share'. Don't neglect/forget/deny your crucial involvement in defining similarities, generalities, differences and identities. You are juggling and grouping/separating your own internal representations. The actual objective objects are not involved, and need not even exist.

Josh:

We are very close. So I certainly agree that all my perceptions depend on my mind. So if I perceive a similarity, that perception depends upon my mind. True enough. What I want to say is that there is a difference between your perception, which depends upon your mind, and that which you perceive -- which may or may not depend upon your mind. For example, I think that I perceive (perhaps indirectly) a computer in front of me. My perception of the computer depends upon my mind, but the computer itself does not. In the same way, I think I perceive that some computers are similar to other computers in some respects. This perception of similarity depends upon my mind, but the similarity itself does not. Just as computers can exist without me, they can have features in common without me.

So the point at issue, then, is whether anything is similar apart from my perception. Or, to put the point from your perspective, the question is whether anything is similar apart from your perception. Seeing this precise point is itself progress, and worth celebrating. :)

Now, just to be sure we are on the same page, then, would you say at least that something can exist apart from your perception?

Thanks for having this exchange with me. I am truly excited about your book. Btw, I have some extra isbn numbers, and I would be happy to give you one if you need it to help you publish your book.

Best wishes,

Josh

Joe:

Hi, and wonderful. This second chemo treatment may need adjustment. It is supposed to be weekly to allow recovery, but this first cycle made my useless and agonized for 6 days. Today is Sunday and I am scheduled for the next tomorrow.

Yes, I can use any help I can get, and am ignorant about publishing. Yes, an ISBN number would be wonderful.

"In the same way, I think I perceive that some computers are similar to other computers in some respects. This perception of similarity depends upon my mind, but the similarity itself does not."

I do appreciate your using the distinction between your subjective perception/model/image of something and the objective thing (if it exists). However, 'similarity' is not objective, it is a mental application, a judgement made, based on a test decided by the comparator. The first of something has no similarity, or does it? If not, then this first something changes in no way, gains nothing and gives nothing when the second something arrives. And if we want to say that a first something already has similarities, we are instantly free to do so by ignoring the aspects of it which denote 'firstness', and instead tabulate the aspects of it that are generic enough to include as many other things as we want. "All is one" is the ultimate similarity application. Some people will spend and earn significant money to distinguish the most absolutely identical objects, based on which one of them was owned by Marilyn Monroe. Similarity is entirely controlled by the criteria chosen by the comparator. Similarity is a declaration of judgement, an *act* of defining a set to which the members must qualify. This is a fundamental tool of thought, but similarity, again, is like beauty, in the eye of the judger. You and I may agree that the grains of sand and computers are similar, but that is more proximally so because you and I are similar than the objects in question, and if you or I wanted to find disagreement, the fastest route would be to find a third opinion, rather than find hidden disagreements between our criteria for similitude. There are always ones who will only want the computer owned by Prince. We could say that these two grains of sand were similar because they *would* (we predict) react the same, in similar circumstances. That of course just kicks the can a little down the alley, begging the question of how we define/construct those 'similar' circumstances. The universe provides us with only one global circumstance at any time, with no repeats, so the similarity of circumstances is also an artifice, subject to the construction/evaluation/declaration of the comparator. Comparison, generalization is the sole and beneficial purview of consciousness/subjectivity, as a heuristic for forming predictions. We do it 'innately' in our subconscious 'plausibility engine', and are biased to do so, testedly, provenly perceiving patterns (similarities) in data that has been mathematically generated to be guaranteed statistically random.

Josh:

So, just to be sure:

1. You would say that something (like me) can exist apart from your mind.

2. You would say that no two things can be similar apart from you mind.

Would you also say that something can have an attribute apart from your mind? For example, could an electron have mass apart from your mind? (I ask because if electrons can have mass, then they can have something in common -- namely, mass -- apart from your mind. And to have something in common is what I mean by "similar.")

Best,

Josh

Joe:

Hi! I've climbed back up temporarily from chemo, and am juggling the hopes of chemo with the unusually draconian effects... I am concentrating on editing my chapters, and am making them more readable and with more integrated insights I hope. Do send the ISBN at your convenience and let me know if there is anything else I need to do besides giving it to a publisher!

And:

I *do* commit on practically invincible faith, to things existing apart from my mind, and wonderfully, such as you! But I am utterly aware that logical surety is a quality which is hermetically sealed and limited to within my mind. The belief in *anything other than a construct/vision in/of my/your mind* involves, eternally, logically, a leap of faith in the positive direction from the jump-off position of Solipsism.

I would say that any two things, by simply being such, initially and definitionally are utterly separate and distinct. Whether any two things can be deemed to be similar is freely and totally a product of the generalization you construct in your mind, which defines/chooses the attributes of a thing that you want to matter when qualifying any thing, in/for the current definition of 'similar'.

And no, a thing is not inherently parsed into attributes. A thing, per se, just *is* 'holistically'. It is, again, the product of a generalizing mind to parse and define attributes, according to the unifying/generalizing efforts of the mind. Indeed, for some world-views(ontologies) there are some things, which for other ontologies are not even a thing. Not long ago, electrons weren't a thing. Physics is the burgeoningly successful integration and testing of theories (generalizations) about what we believe on faith to be that real objective universe out there, sterilely, reliably, independent of our minds. The state of art definitely projects electrons as essentially identical in function (modulo their individual energy state and location etc.), with attributes that map to some specific core generalities of physics like mass.

And two electrons are no different than the case of two general things above. They are utterly, ever distinct and separate, and their similarity is in our declaration that they belong in the same set whose membership criteria we define. If we test two electrons and they behave the same, it is the criteria of the test which defines the set/similarity. Another test can easily find them different. Test-2: Is it bound to an atom which is in turn bound as part of the solid mass which is defined as my sandwich?

Generalizing, classifying, unifying by set, etc. All purely activities of the mind.

Your mind, on its own, and nothing as sure as its contents and imaginations. Nothing besides the creations and imaginings and raw experiences of your mind, are as logically sure as them, certainly not any of your interpretations that posit anything besides you.

The reliability/repeatability of your ideas has to do with the acumen of your memory, and that once you attain a logical surety, such as 'A=A' it is a proven item of logical consistency, a reliable brick from which to synthesize more. None of it's reliability etc.

can ever be evidence, let alone proof of anything beyond your mind, hermetically sealed as we are in our mind, from the strict subjective/objective split perspective. Nor is there, or can there be any evidence of your perfect thought, except when you're thinking it. All thought is private to the mind that generated it. The mind, like the physical universe, is a closed system. It is only by our leap of credulity/faith from where we are, inside our mind, that we trust in our interpretations that there is that other realm we're experiencing.

You are an oasis of beauty. I am out of the woods with this last episode, back home for exploiting the good times. Here is the attached word-doc. The fact that you can articulate in this deep-water field makes the seminal difference in my fundamentally feeling heard, understood, and therefore have something to offer. And do let me know if you have follow-up points and ideas for our last conversation. Here is a blurb I wrote thinking about it.

Reason, honed to it's uttermost reliability, which is to say that therein no desire or need, no matter how fervent will have any purchase or sway on what reality actually is, and that no image or linguistic construct, no matter how sophisticated and self-consistent, no matter how well memorized and recalled, can produce or imply anything more than the image/construct itself, that it can provably lead to nowhere/nothing beyond the private imaginary of the mind where it resides.

We are in deep waters. In fact infinitely deep, in all directions. Our finest water ballet is nevertheless just treading water in place. It can never be as if we jumped out of a plane, and had cleverly taken a ladder with us, so we could then regain altitude at any time, simply by climbing it as needed. It is *only* by credulous faith that we cling to and posit anything else, that we can then bond to, and be affected by, including and most crucially (to me) any real 'we'. For most sentient life forms, this first leap of faith is, precipitately and unconsideredly, to be in touch and reactive to our 'screen of raw inputs', our 5 senses, that they faithfully represent an objective world/realm/universe where we find others.

Think of our logical progressions/conclusions as those ladders we create, along with our hierarchy of ideas/laws/symmetries observed and tended. You (and notably and particularly you!) should take deep credit for the beauty, richness, and reliability of your world view. It is crafted, enriched and beautiful to the credit of your powerful, instant-acting pre-linguistic intuition/aesthetics, not just your sharp rationality. You are as good at (and more core importantly so), at *judging*, at a surpassing fine degree of nuance, as you are in, then, as/if needed/wanted, linguistic/ mathematical articulation at a philosophical perspective.

The clean, utter separation of the objective(public, impersonal) and the subjective(private, personal) provides a Gödel-esque proof of impossibility-of-proof of anything beyond either side, from either side.

I will define the 'no objectivity' hypothesis of Solipsism, as the arguable world view that *everything* is *your* private imagination/dream, that absolutely nothing else exists, nor needs to, except as/when you are imagining it. No brain, no bucket, no real 'we', just you talking to us sock puppets you create, whether you know it or not... The eternal, inexorable, and never logically disprovable possibility of this hypothesis being true means that any other ontology/world view which posits anything other than the one mind of the proposer, has to propose any such other thing as moot, and a matter of faith, buttressed perhaps by anecdote or statistics, but never a destination or delivery of pure inarguable logic.